Elements of
Introducto

Holt Adapted Reader

from *Elements of Literature*
- Adapted Literary Selections
- Poetry Selections
- Adapted Informational Texts

HOLT, RINEHART AND WINSTON
A Harcourt Education Company
Orlando • **Austin** • New York • San Diego • Toronto • London

CREDITS

Executive Editor: Katie Vignery

Senior Editor: Amy Strong

Editor: Nicole Svobodny

Copyediting: Michael Neibergall, *Copyediting Manager;* Kristen Azzara, Mary Malone, *Copyediting Supervisors;* Christine Altgelt, Elizabeth Dickson, Leora Harris, Anne Heausler, Kathleen Scheiner, *Senior Copyeditors;* Emily Force, Julia Thomas Hu, Nancy Shore, *Copyeditors*

Project Administration: Marie Price, *Managing Editor;* Elizabeth LaManna, *Associate Managing Editor;* Janet Jenkins, *Senior Editorial Coordinator;* Christine Degollado, Betty Gabriel, Mark Koenig, Erik Netcher, *Editorial Coordinators*

Permissions: Ann Farrar, *Senior Permissions Editor*

Design: Richard Metzger, Betty Mintz

Production: Beth Prevelige, *Senior Production Manager;* Carol Trammel, *Production Manager;* Leanna Ford, Belinda Barbosa Lopez, Michael Roche, *Senior Production Coordinators;* Dolores Keller, Carol Marunas, *Production Coordinators;* Myles Gorospe, *Production Assistant*

Publishing Services: Laura Likon, *Technical Services Director;* Juan Baquera, *Technical Services Manager;* Margaret Sanchez, *Senior Technical Services Analyst*

Manufacturing: Shirley Cantrell, *Manufacturing Supervisor;* Mark McDonald, *Inventory Analyst;* Amy Borseth, *Manufacturing Coordinator*

Copyright © by Holt, Rinehart and Winston

All rights reserved. No part of this publication may be reproduced or transmitted in any form or by any means, electronic or mechanical, including photocopy, recording, or any information storage and retrieval system, without permission in writing from the publisher.

Requests for permission to make copies of any part of this work should be mailed to the following address: Permissions Department, Holt, Rinehart and Winston, 10801 N. MoPac Expressway, Building 3, Austin, Texas 78759.

Printed in the United States of America

0-03-035709-8

1 2 3 4 5   179   05 04 03

Contents

Skills Table of Contents vii
To the Student viii

Reading Literature and Informational Texts

Just Once — *based on the story by Thomas J. Dygard* 1
Retelling Chart 7

The Stone — *based on the story by Lloyd Alexander* 8
Making Predictions Chart 14
Vocabulary 15

The Bridegroom — *by Alexander Pushkin, translated by D. M. Thomas* 16
Climax: Plot Chart 28
Vocabulary 29

Ta-Na-E-Ka — *based on the story by Mary Whitebird* 30
Conflict Chart 36
Vocabulary 37

The Wind People — *based on the history article by Flo Ota De Lange* 38
Outline Organizer 41

The Bracelet — *based on the short story by Yoshiko Uchida* 42
Point-of-View Chart 48
Vocabulary 49

Wartime Mistakes, Peacetime Apologies — *based on the article by Nancy Day* 50
Taking Notes 53

Everybody Is Different, but the Same Too — *based on the interview with Nilou* 54
Evaluating Conclusions Chart 57

CONTENTS iii

The Emperor's New Clothes	*based on the fairy tale by Hans Christian Andersen* 58
	Theme Chart 63
Uniform Style	*based on the article by Mara Rockliff* 64
	Recognizing Evidence 67
Baucis and Philemon	*based on the myth retold by Olivia Coolidge* 68
	Univeral Themes 72
	Vocabulary 73
One Child's Labor of Love	*based on the news report from 60 Minutes* 74
	Fact and Opinion 77
Separate but Never Equal	*based on the article by Mara Rockliff* 78
	Contrast Chart 81
La Bamba	*based on the story by Gary Soto* 82
	Sequencing .... .87
Medusa's Head	*based on the Greek myth, retold by Olivia Coolidge* 88
	Mythic Hero Web 93
Bringing Tang Home	*based on the article by Gina Spadafori* 95
Where the Heart Is	*based on the article by Sheri Henderson* 97
	Main-Idea Web 99
Brother	*based on the autobiography by Maya Angelou* 100
	Description 104
	Vocabulary 105
All Aboard with Thomas Garrett	*based on the article by Alice P. Miller* 106
	Implied Main Idea Organizer 111

The Mysterious
Mr. Lincoln *based on the biography by Russell Freedman* **112**
Prior-Knowledge Web 117

Lincoln's Humor *based on the article by Louis W. Koenig* **118**
Supporting Assertions 122
Vocabulary 123

Getting Leftovers
Back on the Table *based on the article by Mara Rockliff* **124**
Assertions Web 127

John Henry *Anonymous* . . . . African American song . . . **128**
Questioning the Text 133

The Dog of Pompeii *based on the short story by Louis Untermeyer* **134**
Making Inferences 141

Pet Adoption
Application . . . . application **142**
Veterinarian Registration Form 145

CONTENTS **V**

Skills Table of Contents

Reading Skills

Cause and Effect, 16
Compare and Contrast, 30, 78
Dialogue with the Text, 88
Evaluating Conclusions, 54
Fact and Opinion, 74
Implied Main Idea, 106
Main Idea, 38, 94, 100, 106
Making and Supporting Assertions, 118, 124
Making Generalizations, 58
Making Inferences, 134
Making Predictions, 8, 42

Outlining, 38
Questioning with the Text, 128
Recognizing Connections, 68
Recognizing Evidence, 64
Retelling, xii
Sequencing, 82
Summarizing, 54
Taking Notes, 50
Understanding Applications, 142
Using Prior Knowledge, 112

Literary Skills

Climax, 16
Conflict, xii, 30
Credible Characters, 134
Description, 100
First-Person Point of View, 42
Metaphor, 112
Moral Lessons, 8

Mythic Heroes, 88
Point of View, 42
Refrain, 128
Short Story, 82
Theme, 58, 68
Universal Themes, 68

Vocabulary Skills

Antonyms (Opposites), 102
Context Clues, 12, 32, 62, 71, 86, 92, 123
Interpreting Idioms, 102
Matching Definitions, 15, 29, 37, 49, 73
Multiple Meanings, 66

Prefixes and Suffixes, 70, 120
Synonyms, 105
Using New Words in Sentences, 15, 29, 49, 73
Word Roots, 10, 70, 120

To the Student

A Book for You

Imagine this. A book full of great stories and interesting informational articles. Make it a book that actually tells you to write in it. Fill it with graphic organizers. Make it a size that's easy to carry around. That's *Holt Adapted Reader*—a book created especially for you.

In *Holt Adapted Reader*, you will find two kind of selections—adaptations and original selections.

Adaptations are based on stories or articles that appear in *Elements of Literature*, Introductory Course. Adaptations make the selections more accessible to all readers. You can easily identify any selection that is an adaptation. Just look for the words "based on" in the Table of Contents or selection openers.

Original selections are exactly what appear in *Elements of Literature*, Introductory Course. The poems in this book are examples of original selections. With some poems, you will find helps called **IN OTHER WORDS**. In Other Words paraphrases, or explains, the verses that come before it.

Holt Adapted Reader is designed to accompany *Elements of Literature*. Like *Elements of Literature*, it's designed to help you interact with the literature and informational materials you read.

Learning to Read Literary and Informational Texts

When you read informational materials, you usually read to get the facts. You read mainly to get information that is stated directly on the page. When you read literature, you need to go beyond understanding the words on the page. You need to read between the lines of a poem or story to discover the meaning. No matter what kind of reading you do, *Holt Adapted Reader* will help you practice the skills and strategies you need to become an active and successful reader.

A Walk Through

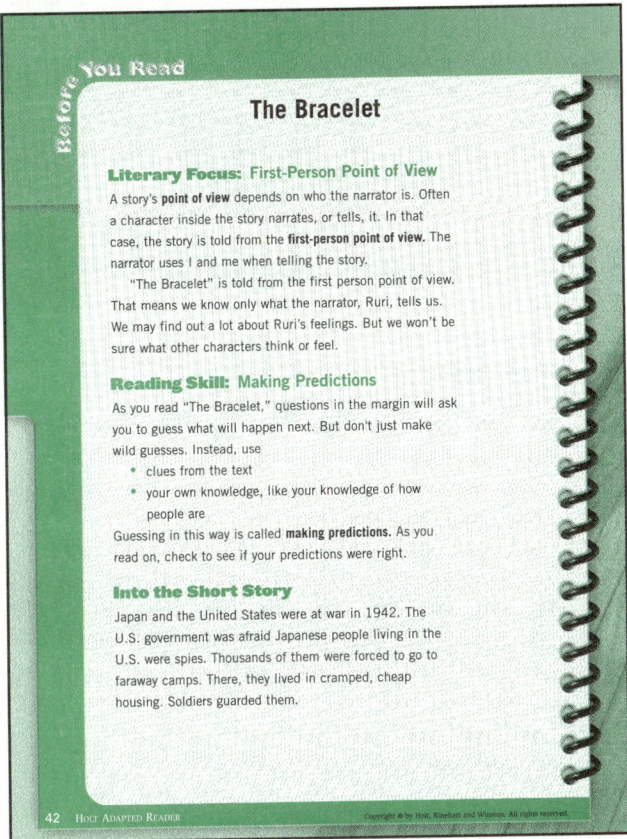

Before You Read
The Before You Read page previews the skill or skills you will practice as you read the selection.
- The **Literary Focus** introduces one literary element—like character or rhyme. This literary element is one you will see in the selection.
- The **Reading Skill** presents a key skill you will need to read the selection.

The Before You Read page also introduces you to the reading selection.
- **Into the Short Story** (or poem, or article) gives you background information. This information will help you understand the selection or its author. It may also help you understand the time period in which the story is set.

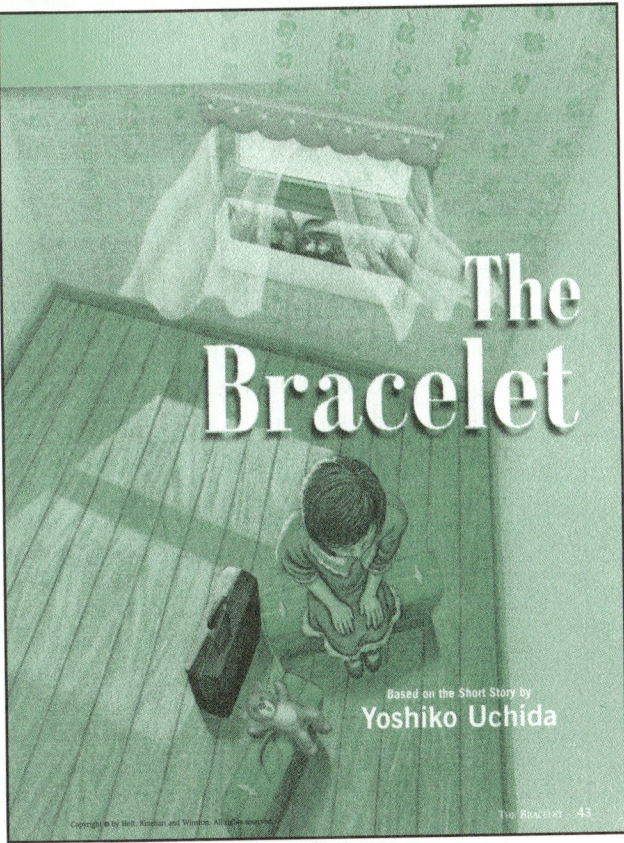

Interactive Selections from *Elements of Literature*
The selections in *Holt Adapted Reader* also appear in *Elements of Literature*, Introductory Course. Most of these selections are adaptations. The selections are reprinted in a single column. They are also printed in larger type to give you the room you need to mark up the text.

TO THE STUDENT ix

A Walk Through

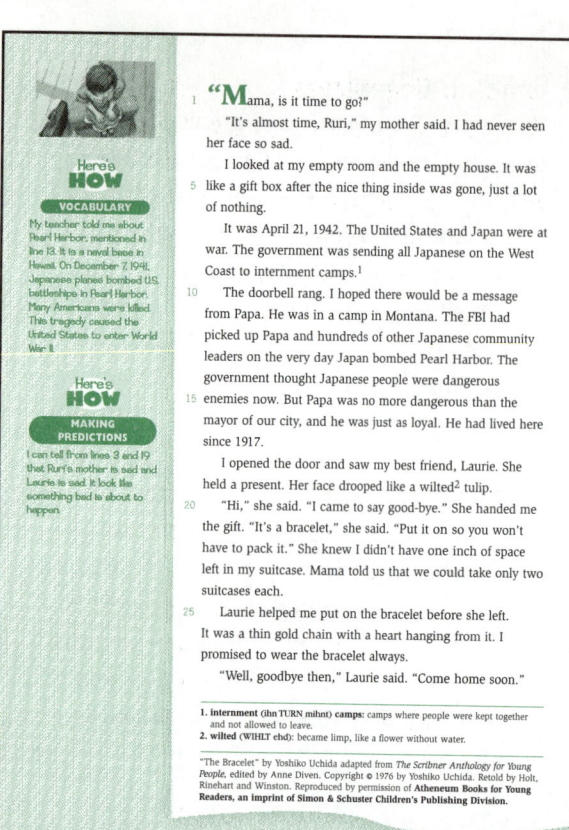

Side Notes

The **Here's HOW** feature shows you how to apply a particular skill to what you are reading. This feature lets you see how another reader might think about the text. You can figure out the focus of a **Here's HOW** by looking in the green oval under the heading. Each **Here's HOW** focuses on a reading skill, a literary skill, or a vocabulary skill.

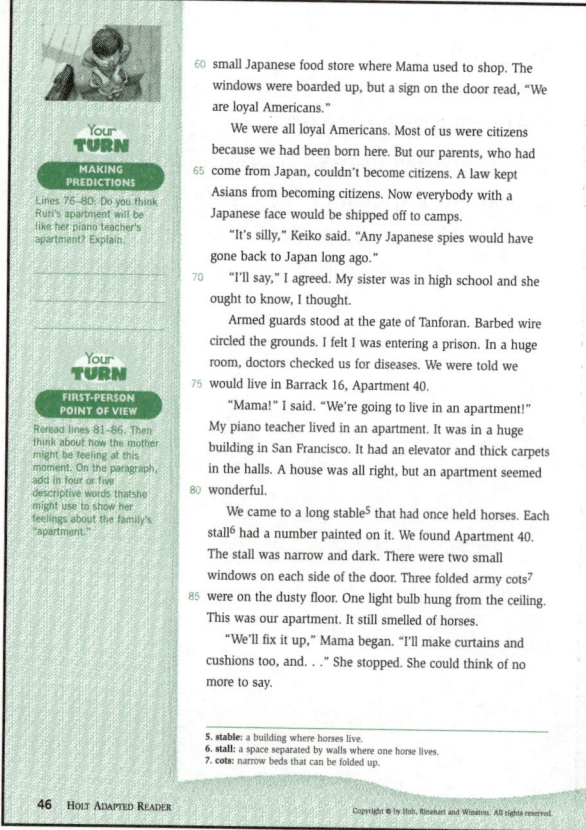

The **Your TURN** feature gives you a chance to practice a skill on your own. Each **Your TURN** focuses on a reading skill, a literary skill, or a vocabulary skill. You might be asked to underline or circle words in the text. You might also be asked to write your responses on lines that are provided for you.

X   TO THE STUDENT

A Walk Through

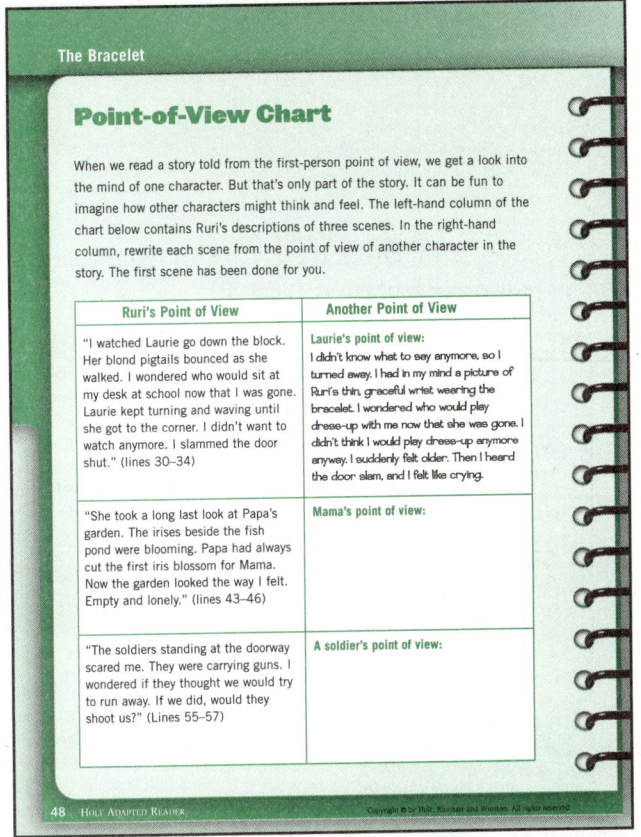

Graphic Organizers
After each selection, **graphic organizers** give you another way to understand the reading or literary focus of the selection. You might be asked to chart the main events of the plot or complete a cause-and-effect chain.

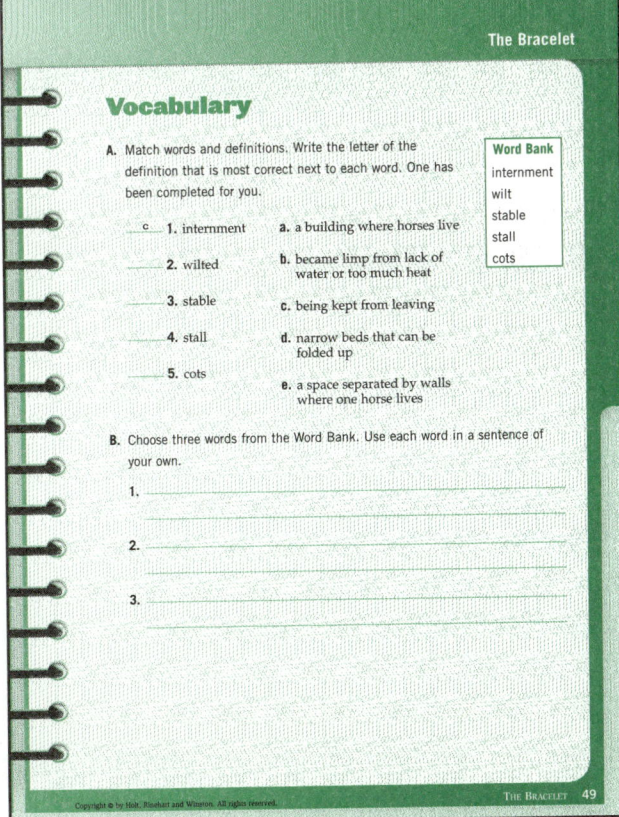

Vocabulary
Vocabulary worksheets appear at the end of some selections. These worksheets check your knowledge of vocabulary words and your understanding of the selection.

TO THE STUDENT   xi

Before You Read

Just Once

Literary Focus: Conflict

Conflict is a struggle between characters and forces. Most of us know a lot about conflict. We want to go to a movie, but our friends want to stay home. We want to play outside, but it's raining. The conflicts begin.

In literature, conflict is often the problem or struggle that makes a story interesting. The diagram below shows three things a story's main character might struggle with.

Reading Skill: Retelling

Retelling is a strategy for understanding a story's plot and conflict. You will start building your retelling of "Just Once" as you answer the on-page questions. You'll put together your complete retelling on page 7.

Into the Story

In this story, Bryan "the Moose" Crawford is a high school football player. He wants to become famous. He tries to get his coach to let him carry the ball, but the coach refuses. This struggle pulls us into the story. It won't let us go until we find out who wins.

JUST ONCE

Based on the Story by
Thomas J. Dygard

RETELLING

The story is called "Just Once." The Moose is probably the main character. The title makes me think of someone really, really wanting to do something—just once. Maybe the Moose wants something.

CONFLICT

I know there's a big conflict in this story. Line 7 says that the Moose is a left tackle—he blocks for other players. But lines 14–15 say that his "hang-up," or problem, is that he wants to carry the ball. That's not his job on the team. I wonder if he'll ever get to carry the ball.

VOCABULARY

I don't know much about football, but I can still figure out what's going on in the story. It's enough to know that the tackle, back, blocker, and lineman are players on the team. The main thing I need to figure out is who carries the ball and who doesn't.

1 Everybody liked the Moose. To his parents he was Bryan. At Bedford City High he was the Moose. He was large and strong. And he was fast on his feet for his size. He had a quick and easy smile. "Sweet," some of the teachers called
5 it. "Nice," others said.

But on the football field, he was neither sweet nor nice. He was just the Bears' strong, fast left tackle. When the Moose blocked somebody, he stayed blocked. When the Moose opened a hole in the line, the hole looked like an
10 open garage door.

The Moose had been on the all-conference team twice. His last year, he was a sure bet[1] for all-state. Many colleges wanted him as a football player. But the Moose had a hang-up.

15 The Moose wanted to carry the ball.

Now, he was not the first player in the line to dream of running for a touchdown. Of hearing fans scream his name.

But most players in the line know they play best there.
20 Football is, after all, a team sport. Everyone plays where he most helps the team. And so most players from the line forget about those dreams.

Not the Moose.

In the sixth game, the Bears were behind 21–17. They
25 had the ball on Mitchell High's five-yard line. It was fourth down,[2] with time running out. In that case, the best back carries the ball behind the best blocker. That meant Jerry Dixon running behind the Moose. With the snap of the ball,

---

1. **sure bet:** certain to be.
2. **fourth down:** In football the team holding the ball is allowed four downs, or attempts to carry the ball forward at least ten yards.

"Just Once" by Thomas J. Dygard adapted from *Ultimate Sports* by Donald R. Gallo. Copyright © 1995 by Thomas Dygard. Retold by Holt, Rinehart and Winston. Reproduced by permission of **Random House Children's Books, a division of Random House, Inc.,** www.randomhouse.com.

the Moose knocked down one lineman. He bumped another
30 aside. He charged another. Jerry did a little jig[3] behind the
Moose. Then Jerry made a touchdown to win the game.

The crowd cheered the touchdown. Then Jerry hugged
the Moose. Jerry knew who had made the touchdown
possible.

35 But it wasn't the Moose's name that everybody was
shouting. The fans were cheering Jerry.

In the dressing room, Coach Williams stopped the Moose.
"Your great blocking did it," he said.

"I want to carry the ball," the Moose said.

40 Coach Williams thought the Moose would say, "Aw, gee,
thanks, Coach," as usual.

"You keep right on blocking, son." The coach moved on.

Moose said no more all week or at the next road game.
45 The Moose wanted to carry the ball for the fans at home. The
next week on the practice field, the Moose went to work. "I
want to carry the ball," he reminded the coach.

"Son, you're great in the line," Coach Williams said. "You
can really block. Let's leave it that way."

50 The Moose went to Dan Blevins, the Bears' quarterback.
Maybe Coach Williams would listen to Dan.

"I heard," Dan said. "But what about the guard? Or even
the center? They might all want to carry the ball. What are
we going to do—take turns? It doesn't work that way."

55 So much for Dan Blevins.

Most of the backfield agreed with Dan. Why should the
Moose carry the ball instead of them? Some of the others
from the line backed the Moose. Maybe they had dreams of
their own.

60 In time the word spread around town. The players by now

---

3. **jig:** a bouncy dance.

RETELLING

In line 39, the Moose tells Coach he wants to carry the ball. What led him to say this? Underline the event that finally pushed the Moose into announcing his wish.

CONFLICT

At first, the Moose's conflict about carrying the ball is with Coach Williams. Then, in lines 50–59, other people join the conflict. Who else is in conflict with the Moose?

_____
_____
_____
_____
_____

JUST ONCE   3

RETELLING

What do you think Coach's attitude is toward the Moose at this point (lines 67–69)?

_____
_____
_____
_____

CONFLICT

Describe the conflict that the Moose faces when the crowd chants, "Give the Moose the ball!" in lines 75–76.

_____
_____
_____
_____
_____

were openly taking sides. Some thought the Moose should carry the ball. Others, like Dan Blevins, held fast.[4] Players from the line should stay there. Backs carry the ball. That's it.

65 Around town, everyone wanted the Moose to carry the ball.

Before the Benton Heights game the coach spoke to the Moose. "This has gone far enough. Fun is fun. A joke is a joke. But let's drop it."

70 "Just once," the Moose pleaded.

Coach Williams looked at the Moose and didn't answer.

The Tigers were easy for the Bears. Everyone knew they would be. The Bears led 28–0 at the half. The Tigers hadn't crossed the fifty-yard line.

75 Sometimes the crowd chanted: "Give the Moose the ball!" The coach seemed mad.

The Moose wondered if the crowd would make the coach give in. Maybe the coach would refuse to give the ball to the Moose just to show everyone who was boss.

80 By the end of the third quarter, the Bears were leading 42–0.

Coach Williams had been using subs since half time. Still the Bears marched on. Early in the fourth quarter, the Bears were on the Tigers' five-yard line. The Bears were ready
85 to score again.

Larry Hinden headed for the field. The Moose thought Larry would take his place. Then Larry told the referee,[5] "Hinden for Holbrook."

Holbrook? The fullback?

90 Leaving the field, Holbrook gave the coach a funny look.

Larry spoke to the team. "Coach says the Moose at fullback. Give him the ball."

---

4. held fast: would not change their minds.
5. referee: someone who judges in sports.

The Moose gave his grin. "Sweet," some of the teachers called it. "Nice," others said.

"I want to do an end run," the Moose said.

Dan looked at the sky. Then he said, "What does it matter?"

The quarterback took the snap from center. He moved back and to his right. He handed the ball to the Moose. The Moose took the ball. He held it in his right hand. So far, so good. He hadn't dropped the ball. Likely both Coach Williams and Dan were surprised. The Moose ran a few steps. He looked ahead. He said aloud, "Whoa!"

Where had all those tacklers come from?

The whole field seemed full of Tigers. They all were moving toward him. They did not look friendly. And there were so many of them. He had faced rough guys in the line. Often one at a time, or maybe two. Not five or six. And all of them heading for him.

The Moose stopped, turned, and ran the other way.

Dan Blevins blocked a Tiger breaking through the line. The Moose wanted to thank him. But he kept going.

His turn had caught the Tigers' defenders going the wrong way. The field before the Moose looked open. But his blockers were going the wrong way, too. Still, the field was clear in front of him. This would be easy. He would score a touchdown.

Then, again—"Whoa!"

Tigers filled the empty space. They all ran toward the Moose. They were low, with their arms spread. They wanted to hit him hard.

The Moose remembered Jerry Dixon slipping between tacklers. How did he do that?

The Moose lowered his shoulder. He ran ahead, into the Tigers. Something hit his left leg. It hurt. Something hit his

Your TURN

RETELLING

The Moose finally gets to carry the ball. How is it different from what he is used to? Re-read lines 105–109.

_____
_____
_____

Your TURN

CONFLICT

What is happening in the Moose's head as he runs with the ball in lines 113–123?

_____
_____
_____
_____
_____
_____
_____

JUST ONCE 5

RETELLING

Finally, the Moose's dream comes true. Do you think carrying the ball has been better or worse than he expected? Explain.

_____
_____
_____
_____
_____

CONFLICT

In the last two lines of the story, the Moose's central conflict ends. Is the ending what you expected? What did you expect to happen?

_____
_____
_____
_____
_____
_____
_____

hip and shoulder. They both hurt. Somebody hung on to him. He knew he was going down. Maybe he was across the goal. He hit the ground hard. Somebody landed on the small of his back.

130   The Moose couldn't move. They had him pinned. Wasn't the referee supposed to get these guys off?

Finally he was free. The Moose, still holding the ball, stood.

He heard the crowd scream. He saw the scoreboard
135 blink.

He had scored.

His teammates slapped him on the shoulder pads. They laughed and shouted.

The Moose grinned. He had a strange, faraway look in his
140 eyes.

He moved off the field. The crowd's roar rang in his ears.

"OK, son?" Coach Williams asked.

The Moose puffed. He took deep breaths. He relived the
145 sight of six Tigers, all headed toward him. He saw again the Tigers closing in on him as he neared his goal.

The Moose glanced at the coach. The Moose took another deep breath. He said, "Never again."

Retelling Chart

One of the best ways to understand a story is to retell it for someone else. The **retelling** strategy lets you do that. Use the chart to put together your retelling notes. Then "retell" the events of "Just Once" aloud to your class.

Retelling Guide	
1. Introduction: Give the title, author, and setting of the story.	
2. Characters: Who is the main character? What does he want? What are the names of other important characters?	
3. Conflict: Why can't the main character get what he wants? How are the other characters blocking or helping the main character?	
4. Complications—The Main Events: What happens as the main character tries to get what he wants?	
5. Climax—The Most Suspenseful Moment: What happens at the moment when the main character finally does (or doesn't) get what he wants?	
6. Resolution: How does the story end?	
7. What Is Your Personal Response?	

Before You Read

The Stone

Literary Focus: Moral Lessons

Most stories have a message. Fairy tales have **morals,** which are messages or lessons about the right way to behave. "The Stone" was written by a modern writer. However, it has the feel, and the moral, of an old fairy tale.

Reading Skill: Making Predictions

When you read a book or watch a movie, do you ever guess what will happen next? If so, you know what it means to make a prediction. Making predictions helps keep your mind awake as you read. To make predictions as you read "The Stone," follow these steps:

read for clues **+** use what you already know about fairy tales **+** remember what you know about the world

Into the Story

Have you ever wished you could be older, right now? In "The Stone," the adult character has the opposite wish: he wants to *stop* growing older. Read to find out what happens when his wish comes true.

The Stone

BASED ON THE STORY BY
Lloyd Alexander

Here's HOW
VOCABULARY

Sickly (line 2) — sounds like "sick." Maybe the old man doesn't look very healthy. That must be why Maibon is so upset by seeing him.

Here's HOW
MAKING PREDICTIONS

I don't think the dwarf in the field is an ordinary person. Maibon calls him one of the "Fair Folk." Maybe that means he's going to use magical fairy powers. But I always thought fairies were cute, like Tinkerbell!

1 **O**ne day a man named Maibon was driving down the road on his horse and cart when he saw a <u>sickly</u> old man. Maibon shook his head at such a sad sight and went on his way home. When he got home, he said to his wife, Modrona:

5 "Ah, ah, what a sorry thing it is to grow old. When I think that this might happen to me, too!"

"Stop looking for trouble," answered Modrona. "Take care of your field, or we'll have no food."

Maibon sighed and did as his wife asked. Although it was
10 a lovely day, Maibon took no pleasure in it. None of his tools seemed to cut the way they used to. The sun didn't seem to shine as bright.

"As for me," went on Maibon, "I'm in even worse shape. When I go to bed, my eyes are so heavy I can't hold them
15 open. As I grow older, things will only get worse!"

As he was complaining, Maibon noticed something in a corner of the field. He dropped his ax and opened his mouth in surprise.

There he saw a redheaded dwarf who was struggling to
20 get his leg from under a log. When the dwarf saw Maibon, he shouted, "Well, come on! Don't stand there like an idiot. Help me get loose!"

Maibon scratched his head: "Well, now, just a moment, friend. The way you look—I'm thinking you might be one of
25 the Fair Folk."

"Oh, smart!" Doli, the dwarf, snapped back. "Of course I am! Enough talking. Get a move on. My leg's going to sleep."

Maibon got excited. "If a man does the Fair Folk a good turn, " he cried, "they say he must return the favor."

"The Stone" adapted from *The Foundling and Other Tales of Prydain* by Lloyd Alexander. Copyright © 1973, 2002 by Lloyd Alexander. Retold by Holt, Rinehart and Winston. Reproduced by permission of **Henry Holt and Company, LLC.** Electronic format by permission of **Brandt & Hochman Literary Agents, Inc.**

30 Doli agreed to grant Maibon a wish if Maibon would help free him. Maibon pulled and chopped away at the log as fast as he could. He freed the dwarf.

Doli let out a sigh of relief and said:

"All right. You've done your work; you'll have your
35 reward. What do you want?"

"I've heard that you Fair Folk have magic stones that can keep a man young forever. That's what I want."

Doli snorted. "I might have known you'd pick something like that. You humans have it all wrong. There's nothing we
40 can do to make a man young again. Those stones only keep you from getting older."

"Just as good!" Maibon exclaimed. "That's what I want!"

Doli hesitated[1] and frowned. "Those stones—we'd sooner not give them away. There's a difficulty—"

45 Maibon broke in. "I told you what I want, and that's what I'll have."

Doli shrugged and handed Maibon a large stone. Then, he jumped up and ran away.

Laughing, Maibon hurried back to his house. There he
50 told his wife what had happened and showed her the stone. His wife was not happy and called him a fool for asking the dwarf for a stone.

Disappointed, Maibon began thinking his wife was right. He threw the stone into the fireplace.

55 But, when Maibon woke up the next morning, he patted his cheeks in amazement. "My beard!" he cried to his wife. "It hasn't grown!"

"Don't talk to me about beards," his wife replied. "There's trouble enough in the chicken roost. Those eggs should have
60 been hatched by now."

---

1. **hesitated** (HEHZ uh tayt ehd): to wait a moment, because of feeling unsure.

MORAL LESSON

In lines 38-41, Doli tries to warn Maibon about making the wrong wish. Maibon is probably going to have to learn a lesson the hard way. I wonder what will go wrong?

MAKING PREDICTIONS

Underline the two things that are unusual when Maibon gets up in the morning (lines 55–60). What other unusual things might Maibon find as the day goes on?

THE STONE 11

Your TURN

VOCABULARY

If a calf is a baby cow, what does it mean to say a cow has not *calved* (line 74)? Hint: Use the clue in line 66.

_____
_____

MORAL LESSON

Re-read lines 79–81. What does this tell you about making wishes?

_____
_____
_____

Maibon went to the fireplace to pick out the stone. "Let the chickens worry about that," answered Maibon. "Wife, don't you see what great thing has happened to me? I'm not a minute older than I was yesterday."

65 "And the cow!" Modrona cried. "She's long past due and still hasn't given birth to a calf!"

"Don't bother me with cows and chickens," replied Maibon. "They'll be all right, in time. As for time, I've got all the time in the world!"

70 When Maibon went out to his field, he was surprised to see that not one of the seeds he had planted there had sprouted.

Some days went by and still the eggs had not hatched. The cow had not calved. The wheat had not sprouted. And 75 now Maibon saw that his apple tree showed no sign of even the smallest, greenest fruit.

His wife blamed the stone. She told Maibon to get rid of it. Maibon replied, "The season's slow, that's all." His wife kept at him. Finally, Maibon threw the stone out the window.

80 The next morning, though, he found the stone sitting on the window sill.

Now Maibon's baby was having trouble. He was cranky from teething, but no tooth was to be seen! Maibon's wife begged her husband to get rid of the stone. This time, Maibon 85 dug a shallow hole and put the stone into it. But the next day the stone sat glittering² above the ground.

Time went by with nothing growing or changing. Maibon grew upset. "Nothing's moving along as it should," he groaned. "There's nothing to look forward to, nothing to 90 show for my work."

Maibon tried to destroy the stone, but no matter what he did, the stone kept coming back. At last, he decided to bury

---

2. **glittering** (GLIHT ehr ihng): sparkling.

12 HOLT ADAPTED READER   Copyright © by Holt, Rinehart and Winston. All rights reserved.

the stone again, this time deeper than before. He picked up his shovel and hurried to the field. As he was running to the field, he saw the dwarf sitting on a stump.

"You should have warned me about the stone!" Maibon shouted at the dwarf.

"I did," Doli shouted back. "You wouldn't listen. Now take my advice. Get rid of that stone, and quickly."

"What do you think I've been trying to do?" blurted Maibon. "It keeps coming back to me whatever I do!"

"That's because you really didn't want to give it up."

"No, no!" cried Maibon. "I want no more of it. Whatever may happen, let it happen. That's better than nothing happening at all."

"If you mean that," answered Doli, "toss the stone onto the ground right there at the stump. Then go home."

Maibon threw down the stone and ran home as fast as he could. He was so happy to see that his field was covered with green blades of wheat and that the apple tree was heavy with fruit. He ran into the house. His wife told him the good news—the hen hatched her chicks; the cow bore her calf. And Maibon laughed with delight when he saw the first tooth in the baby's mouth.

Maibon and his children and grandchildren lived for many years. Maibon was as proud of his long white beard as he had been of his strong body.

"Stones are all right in their way," said Maibon. "But the trouble with them is, they don't grow."

MAKING PREDICTIONS

Will Maibon succeed in getting rid of the stone this time? Explain your answer.

_____
_____
_____
_____

VOCABULARY

What does *bore* mean in line 112? (Hint: Look back at line 66. What do you think has changed here?)

_____
_____
_____

THE STONE 13

The Stone

Making Predictions

As you read "The Stone," you learned how to use clues to make predictions about what might happen next. Now let's review those predictions.

Read each scene from the story in the left-hand column below. These passages were the topics of the Here's How and Your Turns on making predictions (pages 10, 11, and 13). In the middle column, write what actually happened next in the story. Were the predictions you made correct? If so, how did you guess? In the right-hand column, identify the text clue (or real-world knowledge) you used to make the prediction. If the prediction was incorrect, in the same column identify a text clue that pointed to what really happened.

Passage from the Story	What Happened Next	Clue (or Real-World Knowledge) That Predicted What Happened
1. Maibon meets a dwarf in the field. He helps free the dwarf (who is actually one of the "Fair Folk") from beneath a fallen log. (lines 16–27)	The dwarf, Doli, does have magic powers: He grants Maibon a wish.	"Fair Folk" sounded like "fairy"; I knew that fairies had magical powers.
2. The next morning, Maibon finds his beard hasn't grown and the chickens' eggs haven't hatched. (lines 55–60)		
3. Maibon tells Doli he longs to be rid of the stone. (lines 96–105)		

Vocabulary

A. Match words and definitions. Write the letter of the correct definition on the line next to each word. The first one has been done for you.

___c___ **1.** sickly

_____ **2.** hesitated

_____ **3.** calved

_____ **4.** glittering

_____ **5.** bore

a. sparkling

b. gave birth to

c. not in good health

d. gave birth to a calf

e. waited a moment, due to feeling unsure

B. Choose two words from the list above. Use each word in a sentence.

1. _____

_____

2. _____

_____

Before You Read

The Bridegroom

Literary Focus: Climax

The most exciting part of a story is called the **climax.** This is the peak of the story. Everything in the story leads to this moment. At the climax, you find out for sure what will happen to the characters.

Reading Skill: Cause and Effect

"Why did this happen?" When you ask this question, you are wondering about a *cause.* A **cause** makes something happen.

"What's the result of this event?" When you ask this question, you are wondering about an *effect.* An **effect** is the result of a cause. Stories are usually a series of causes and their effects.

Into the Poem

Alexander Pushkin is often called the father of modern Russian literature. Many of Pushkin's writings focus on Russian settings and folk tales. His 1825 poem "The Bridegroom" is based on a folk tale. In the tale, a young woman witnesses a terrible crime. At first, she doesn't tell anyone about the crime. Then she realizes that the man who committed the crime might become her bridegroom. What will happen on their wedding day? Will the young woman be her bridegroom's next victim? Read the poem to find out!

The Bridegroom

BY
Alexander Pushkin

CAUSE AND EFFECT

Why was Natasha missing for three days? I want to keep reading to find out the *cause* of Natasha's disappearance.

CAUSE AND EFFECT

Re-read lines 1–8. Then, fill in the cause-and-effect chart below.

Cause: Something happened to Natasha. (We don't know what.)

Effect (and new cause):

_____

_____

Effect (and new cause): Natasha's parents ask her many questions.

Effect:

_____

_____

1   For three days Natasha,
     The merchant's daughter,
     Was missing. The third night,
     She ran in, distraught.[1]
5   Her father and mother
     Plied[2] her with questions.
     She did not hear them,
     She could hardly breathe.

IN OTHER WORDS Natasha is the daughter of a businessman. She has been missing for three days. When she returns home, her parents ask her many questions. She is too upset to answer them.

     Stricken with foreboding[3]
10   They pleaded, got angry,
     But still she was silent;
     At last they gave up.
     Natasha's cheeks regained
     Their rosy color.
15   And cheerfully again
     She sat with her sisters.

     Once at the shingle-gate[4]
     She sat with her friends
     —And a swift troika[5]
20   Flashed by before them;
     A handsome young man

---

1. **distraught** (dih STRAWT): extremely troubled.
2. **plied** (plyd): addressed urgently, without letting up.
3. **foreboding** (for BOHD ihng): feeling that something bad will happen.
4. **shingle-gate:** gate to the beach (a shingle is a pebbly beach).
5. **troika** (TROY kuh): Russian sleigh or carriage drawn by three horses.

"The Bridegroom" from *The Bronze Horseman and Other Poems* by Alexander Pushkin, translated by D. M. Thomas. Translation copyright © 1982 by D. M. Thomas. Reproduced by permission of **John Johnson Ltd.**

Stood driving the horses;
Snow and mud went flying,
Splashing the girls.

IN OTHER WORDS   Natasha becomes her normal self again. One day Natasha is sitting with her friends near a gate. A handsome young man rushes by in a carriage. As the carriage passes, it splashes the girls with snow and mud.

25 He gazed as he flew past,
    And Natasha gazed.
    He flew on. Natasha froze.
    Headlong she ran home.
    "It was he! It was he!"
30 She cried. "I know it!
    I recognized him! Papa,
    Mama, save me from him!"

IN OTHER WORDS   The man looks at the girls, and Natasha looks at him. Natasha freezes in fear. She runs straight home. She tells her parents that she recognized the man. She begs her parents to save her from this man.

    Full of grief and fear,
    They shake their heads, sighing.
35 Her father says: "My child,
    Tell me everything.
    If someone has harmed you,
    Tell us . . . even a hint."
    She weeps again and
40 Her lips remain sealed.

Here's HOW

CLIMAX

Natasha says she recognizes the man in the carriage (line 31). I bet this man has something to do with why Natasha was missing for three days. Maybe I'll find out later, at the climax. The excitement is building!

Your TURN

CLIMAX

You probably have many questions about what will happen in the poem. Most of these questions will be answered at the climax. List two of your questions on the lines below:

1. _____
   _____
   _____
   _____

2. _____
   _____
   _____
   _____

THE BRIDEGROOM   19

IN OTHER WORDS Natasha's parents are very sad and afraid. Her father begs Natasha to tell him what happened, or at least give him a hint. Natasha won't say a word.

The next morning, the old
Matchmaking woman
Unexpectedly calls and
Sings the girl's praises;
45 Says to the father: "You
Have the goods and I
A buyer for them:
A handsome young man.

IN OTHER WORDS The next morning, a matchmaker visits Natasha's family. The matchmaker says a lot of good things about Natasha and thinks she will make a good wife. The matchmaker knows a young man who will make a good husband for Natasha.

"He bows low to no one,
50 he lives like a lord
With no debts nor worries;
He's rich and he's generous,
Says he will give his bride,
On their wedding-day,
55 A fox-fur coat, a pearl,
Gold rings, brocaded[6] dresses.

"Yesterday, out driving,
He saw your Natasha;
Shall we shake hands

---

6. **brocaded** (broh KAYD ehd): having a raised design woven into the fabric.

Here's HOW

VOCABULARY

I've never heard of a *matchmaking woman* (line 42), but I know what a *matchmaker* is. A *matchmaker* finds husbands for wives, and wives for husbands. She makes matches, or pairs people up. I think *matchmakers* are very important in societies where marriages are arranged. I've heard that in arranged marriages, sometimes couples don't even know each other before they get married!

Your TURN

VOCABULARY

Re-read lines 45–48. The matchmaker calls the young man in the carriage a "buyer." What are the "goods" he wants to "buy"? Explain your answer. (Hint: Think about the matchmaker's job.)

_____
_____
_____
_____

20 HOLT ADAPTED READER

60 And get her to church?"
The woman starts to eat
A pie, and talks in riddles,
While the poor girl
Does not know where to look.

IN OTHER WORDS The matchmaker tries to get Natasha's father to agree to the marriage. She says that the man is rich and generous. When this man gets married, he'll give his wife many beautiful things. This man saw Natasha yesterday when he was out driving. While the matchmaker talks, Natasha becomes very nervous.

65 "Agreed," says her father;
"Go in happiness
To the altar, Natasha;
It's dull for you here;
A swallow should not spend
70 All its time singing,
It's time for you to build
A nest for your children."

IN OTHER WORDS Natasha's father agrees to the marriage. He compares Natasha's life to a bird's. Eventually a bird needs to build a nest for its babies. Natasha, too, should start a family of her own.

Natasha leaned against
The wall and tried
75 To speak—but found herself
Sobbing; she was shuddering
And laughing. The matchmaker

Here's HOW

CAUSE AND EFFECT

I can see the following series of causes and their effects:

Cause: The young man sees Natasha by the gate.

Effect (and new cause): The young man tells the matchmaker he wants to marry Natasha. (We don't see that in the poem, but I can guess that's what happened.)

Effect: The matchmaker visits Natasha's family.

Your TURN

CAUSE AND EFFECT

What kind of **effect** does the matchmaker's visit have on Natasha? Underline the lines that describe her reaction. What do you think Natasha is feeling?

_____
_____
_____
_____

THE BRIDEGROOM 21

Poured out a cup of water,
Gave her some to drink,
80 Splashed some in her face.

IN OTHER WORDS Natasha is upset. She starts to shake and then laughs. To calm her down, the matchmaker splashes some water on Natasha's face.

Her parents are distressed.
Then Natasha recovered,
And calmly she said:
"Your will be done. Call
85 My bridegroom to the feast,
Bake loaves for the whole world,
Brew sweet mead[7] and call
The law to the feast."

IN OTHER WORDS Natasha calms down. She tells her parents that she'll do what they want. She tells them to start preparing food and drinks for the wedding party. She also asks them to invite the police.

"Of course, Natasha, angel!
90 You know we'd give our lives
To make you happy!"
They bake and they brew;
The worthy guests come,
The bride is led to the feast,
95 Her maids sing and weep;
Then horses and a sledge

---

7. **mead** (meed): alcoholic drink made from honey and water.

Here's HOW
CLIMAX

I'm surprised that Natasha agrees to marry that creepy guy! (lines 84–85) She's obviously afraid of him. Maybe she has something planned. Well, I'll find out soon. I'm getting closer and closer to the climax!

Your TURN
CAUSE AND EFFECT

Natasha asks her parents to make bread (line 86) and prepare drinks (line 87) for the wedding. In lines 87–88, she also asks for something else. Underline this strange request. Then, try to guess the **cause** of this unusual action. Write your answer below.

_____
_____
_____
_____
_____

22 HOLT ADAPTED READER

With the groom—and all sit.
The glasses ring and clatter,
The toasting-cup is passed

100 From hand to hand in tumult,[8]
The guests are drunk.

IN OTHER WORDS Natasha's parents prepare for the party. Guests come. The bridesmaids lead Natasha to the party. The groom arrives on a sled pulled by horses. Everyone drinks, makes toasts, and gets drunk.

BRIDEGROOM
"Friends, why is my fair bride
Sad, why is she not
105 Feasting and serving?"

The bride answers the groom:
"I will tell you why
As best I can. My soul
Knows the rest, day and night
110 I weep; an evil dream
Oppresses me." Her father
Says: "My dear child, tell us
What your dream is."

IN OTHER WORDS The bridegroom asks why Natasha is so sad. She tells everyone she's been having a bad dream. Her father asks her to tell them her dream.

"I dreamed," she says, "that I
115 Went into a forest,

---

8. **tumult** (TOO muhlt): noisy commotion.

Here's HOW
CLIMAX

OK. We're getting to the climax! This isn't the kind of physical fight between the good guy and the bad guy like on TV, though. Natasha and the bridegroom are just talking. I think Natasha is going to tell everyone what happened to her when she went missing for three days.

Your TURN
CLIMAX

Why do you think Natasha tells her experience as a dream? How does that add to the suspense, the excitement?

_____
_____
_____
_____
_____
_____
_____
_____
_____
_____

Your TURN

CLIMAX

The author builds up excitement by drawing out the climax of the poem. The bridegroom talks, and then Natasha answers. Re-read lines 103—132. Then, in the lines below, sum up what happens.

1. The bridegroom says _____ _____ _____

Natasha answers _____ _____ _____ _____

2. The bridegroom says _____ _____ _____

Pay attention to how the bridegroom interprets Natasha's dream.

It was late and dark;
The moon was faintly
Shining behind a cloud;
I strayed from the path;
120 Nothing stirred except
The tops of the pine trees.

"And suddenly, as if
I was awake, I saw
A hut. I approach the hut
125 And knock at the door
—Silence. A prayer on my lips
I open the door and enter.
A candle burns. All
Is silver and gold."

IN OTHER WORDS Natasha tells them her dream: She goes out walking in the forest one night and gets lost. Suddenly, she sees a little house. She knocks at the door, but no one answers. Natasha is scared, but she goes into the house. Inside, a candle is burning. The house is decorated with silver and gold.

130 BRIDEGROOM
"What is bad about that?
It promises wealth."

BRIDE
"Wait, sir, I've not finished.
135 Silently I gazed
on the silver and gold,
The cloths, the rugs, the silks

24 HOLT ADAPTED READER

From Novgorod,⁹ and I
Was lost in wonder.

140 "Then I heard a shout
And a clatter of hoofs . . .
Someone has driven up
To the porch. Quickly
I slammed the door and hid
145 Behind the stove. Now
I hear many voices . . .
Twelve young men come in,

IN OTHER WORDS The bridegroom thinks that Natasha's dream means that she'll be wealthy in the future. However, Natasha says she is not finished telling her dream. She says that while she is admiring the house, a group of twelve young men arrive. Natasha hides behind the stove.

"And with them is a girl,
Pure and beautiful.
150 They've taken no notice
Of the ikons,¹⁰ they sit
To the table without
Praying or taking off
Their hats. At the head,
155 The eldest brother,
At his right, the youngest;
At his left, the girl.
Shouts, laughs, drunken clamor . . ."¹¹

---

9. **Novgorod:** city in the northwestern part of Russia.
10. **ikons:** images of Christ, the Virgin, and saints, used in the Eastern Orthodox Church (also spelled *icons*).
11. **clamor** (KLAM uhr): loud noise.

Here's HOW

VOCABULARY

How does Natasha hide behind a stove? (line 145) That's not possible! Well, maybe it's one of those old-fashioned wood-burning stoves. Those stoves don't rest directly against the wall. Yeah, she could hide behind one of those.

Your TURN

CAUSE AND EFFECT

The men's behavior shows that they have no respect. Re-read lines 150–154. Then, fill in the sentences below:

1. The men don't notice

_____

2. They sit down without

_____

3. They don't take off

_____

What **effect** do you imagine this behavior has on Natasha?

_____

_____

Your TURN

VOCABULARY

The word *betokens* (line 160) means "be a sign of, show." What word did the bridegroom use when he told Natasha that the silver and gold in the hut meant that she'd be rich? (Hint: Re-read line 132.) Write your answer below.

_____

Your TURN

VOCABULARY

The word *din* (line 163) means "loud noise." Circle the word in line 164 that gives you a clue to what *din* means. Underline the word in line 158 that has a similar meaning to *din*.

Your TURN

CLIMAX

Who killed the girl in the hut? Can you guess why he cuts off her right hand?

_____
_____
_____

IN OTHER WORDS Natasha continues telling her dream. She says that the men have a beautiful young girl with them. The men and the girl sit down at the table. The men make a lot of noise and get drunk.

BRIDEGROOM
160 "That betokens merriment."

BRIDE
"Wait sir, I've not finished.
The drunken din goes on
And grows louder still.
165 Only the girl is sad.

"She sits, silent, neither
Eating nor drinking;
But sheds tears in plenty;
The eldest brother
170 Takes his knife and, whistling,
Sharpens it; seizing her by
The hair he kills her
And cuts off her right hand."

IN OTHER WORDS The bridegroom tells Natasha that her dream means that she'll have fun in the future. However, Natasha says she's not finished telling her dream. She says that in her dream, the girl is not having fun. She's not eating or drinking. She's crying. Then, one of the men takes out a knife and kills the girl. He cuts off her right hand.

"Why," says the groom, "this
175 Is nonsense! Believe me,
My love, your dream is not evil."
She looks him in the eyes.
"And from whose hand
Does this ring come?"
180 The bride said. The whole throng
Rose in silence.

With a clatter the ring
Falls, and rolls along
The floor. The groom blanches,[12]
185 Trembles. Confusion . . .
"Seize him!" the law commands.
He's bound, judged, put to death.
Natasha is famous!
Our song at an end.

IN OTHER WORDS The bridegroom says the dream doesn't mean anything. Natasha points out that the ring he gave her comes from the dead girl's hand. Everyone looks. The ring falls and rolls along the floor. The bridegroom turns white with fear. The police arrest the bridegroom. He's tried, convicted, and put to death.

---

12. **blanches** (BLANCH ihz): turns pale.

Your TURN

CAUSE AND EFFECT

Re-read lines 180–181. What is the **effect** of Natasha's story on the wedding guests?

Your TURN

CLIMAX

What moment would you say is the **climax** of the poem? Describe what you see happening at that moment.

The Bridegroom

Climax: Plot Chart

Now that you've finished reading "The Bridegroom," think back to the main events in the poem. Then, fill in the plot chart below with the key events that lead to the exciting **climax**. If you'd like, you might want to draw some little pictures to illustrate some of the events or the climax itself.

Climax: _____

Event #4: _____

Event #3: _____

End of story: The bridegroom is put to death, and Natasha becomes famous.

Event #2: _____

Event #1: Natasha witnesses a terrible crime.

Vocabulary

Match each word in the word bank at right with its correct definition below. Write the matching word on the blank in front of the correct definition. Then, use the word in a sentence of your own. Write your sentence on the blank lines after the definition. The third one has been done for you.

Word Bank
distraught (line 4)
foreboding (line 9)
tumult (line 100)
din (line 163)
blanches (line 184)

1. _____ noisy commotion

2. _____ feeling that something bad is going to happen

3. blanches   turns pale
   Every time my mother sees the gas bill, she blanches from the shock.

4. _____ upset

5. _____ loud noise

Ta-Na-E-Ka

Literary Focus: Conflict

Conflict is a struggle between characters or forces. Here are some examples: when you disagree with a friend; when you dislike a school rule; when a thunderstorm ruins your picnic; and when you're confused about a choice.

Whew! Conflict is everywhere—even in the stories you read. But, if you think about it, conflict keeps life and literature exciting. A story without conflict is likely to be dull!

Reading Skill: Compare and Contrast

Comparing shows how two things are the same. **Contrasting** shows how two things are different. To compare and contrast two things, ask yourself these questions:

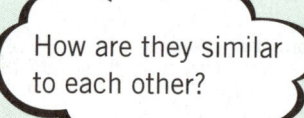

- How are they similar to each other?
- How are they different from each other?

Into the Story

This story is about a girl whose beliefs put her in conflict with her family. Her family follows the traditions of a group of American Indians known as the Kaw. One of these traditions is a test of bravery, the Ta-Na-E-Ka.

The girl's test is to spend five days alone in the woods. Conflict first arises because she sees no reason to take the test. She also does not understand the tradition behind it.

Ta-Na-E-Ka

Based on the Story by
Mary Whitebird

Here's HOW

VOCABULARY

I don't know what *coming-of-age* in line 8 means. But there are clues in the story. Lines 8-10 say it's when you're old enough to show you're a warrior or to become a woman. I'll bet *coming-of-age* means you're old enough to become an adult. I checked in a dictionary, and I was right!

Here's HOW

CONFLICT

I see how conflict works. In lines 1-15, Mary and her cousin Roger have a conflict. They disagree with Mary's mother and grandfather. The adults want Mary and Roger to follow tradition. Mary and Roger disagree. They say that no one follows the old ways now.

Your TURN

CONFLICT

Someone who is not in Mary's family supports the coming-of-age tradition. Re-read lines 16-19 and circle this person's name.

---

1 **A**s my Ta-Na-E-Ka birthday neared, I had bad dreams. I was reaching the age when Kaw Indians take part in Ta-Na-E-Ka. Well, not all Kaws. But my grandfather stuck to the old ways. He was one of the last living Indians who'd
5 fought the U.S. Army. (He died in 1953, when he was eighty-one.) At age eleven, he was wounded at Rose Creek.

Eleven was a magic word among the Kaws. It was the time of Ta-Na-E-Ka, the coming-of-age time. At eleven a boy could prove himself a warrior. A girl took the first steps to
10 womanhood.

"I don't want to be a warrior," my cousin Roger told me. "I'm going to become an accountant."[1]

"It won't be as bad as you think, Mary," my mother said. "Once you've gone through it, you'll never forget it. You'll be
15 proud."

I even talked to my teacher, Mrs. Richardson, a white woman. I thought she would side with me. She didn't.

"All of us have rituals,"[2] she said. "Don't look down on your roots."[3]

20 Roots! I did not plan to keep living on a reservation.[4] But I've always thought that the Kaw started women's liberation.[5] Some other subtribes of the Sioux Nation required men and women to eat separately. But the Kaw men and women ate together. A Kaw woman could refuse a marriage offer. The
25 wisest women often joined in leadership. Also, "Good Woman," a superhero, is the star of most Kaw stories. And

---

1. **accountant** (uh KOWN tuhnt): someone who checks to be sure financial records are correct.
2. **rituals** (RIHCH yoo uhlz): traditions, ceremonies.
3. **roots:** ancestors and their culture and history.
4. **reservation:** land set aside for use by American Indians.
5. **women's liberation:** the struggle for equality between men and women.

"Ta-Na-E-Ka" by Mary Whitebird adapted from *Scholastic Voice*, December 13, 1973. Copyright © 1973 by **Scholastic, Inc.** Retold by Holt, Rinehart and Winston. Reproduced by permission of the publisher.

girls as well as boys go through Ta-Na-E-Ka. The ritual tests how well a person can get along alone.

My grandfather told us that in the past, children were painted white and sent out alone. They had to stay until the paint wore off, about eighteen days. They lived on food they found or caught. They faced enemies: white soldiers and other Indians.

In 1947, Roger and I had it a little easier. We went to the woods for five days. We weren't painted white. We got to wear swimming suits. We did have to find our own food and face the cold. Grandfather taught us how to eat a grasshopper.

I had my own ideas about food. I borrowed five dollars from Mrs. Richardson. I would baby-sit to pay her back.

Roger and I went to the woods together. But we had to stay in separate parts. We couldn't be in touch with each other.

I chose to be near the river. I wanted to sleep in a boat, but I didn't find one.

I tasted a bitter berry I found. I spit it out and a rabbit ate it. Then, I found a place that sold food. I ordered a hamburger and milkshake. I spent forty-five cents of my five dollars.

While I was eating, I had a grand idea. I could sleep here. I unlocked a window in the ladies' room and returned that night. The room was warm. I helped myself to milk and pie. I'd leave money for the food. I planned to get out early before the owner returned.

"What are you doing here, kid?"

It was a man's voice.

It was morning. I'd overslept. I was scared.

"Hold it, kid. You lost? You must be from the reservation. Your folks must be worried sick about you. Do they have a phone?" Ernie, the owner, asked.

Here's HOW

COMPARE AND CONTRAST

In lines 29-38, I can already see that Mary and Roger have it easier than kids in the past. The young people being tested used to be painted white, and they faced enemies. Mary and Roger aren't painted. And they don't have to face enemies.

Your TURN

COMPARE AND CONTRAST

Mary does not plan to do Ta-Na-E-Ka in the old way. She tells of her new plan in lines 48-52. What is her new plan?

_____
_____
_____
_____
_____
_____
_____
_____
_____

Your TURN

COMPARE AND CONTRAST

Mary's feelings about Ta-Na-E-Ka have changed. What are her feelings when she explains the test to Ernie in lines 66–68?

_____
_____
_____
_____

Here's HOW

CONFLICT

Mary really has learned a lot from her Ta-Na-E-Ka. But I can see in lines 83-85 that she's afraid her family won't see how much she's learned. She doesn't look hungry or like she's had to fight off any animals.

"Yes," I answered. "But don't call them." I shook with cold.

The man made me hot chocolate. I told him why I was on my own.

"I've lived by the reservation all my life. I never heard of this test before. Pretty silly thing to do to a kid," he said.

I'd thought that for months. But when he said it, I got angry. "It isn't silly. Kaws have done this for hundreds of years. All my family went through this test. It's why the Kaw are great warriors."

"OK, great warrior," he laughed. "You can stay if you want." He tossed me clothes that people had left on boats. "Find something to keep you warm."

The sweater was loose, but it felt good. I felt good. And I'd found a new friend. Most important, I was surviving Ta-Na-E-Ka.

I stayed at Ernie's for five days. Mornings I went into the woods. I watched the animals and picked flowers. I'd never felt better. I watched the sun rise on the Missouri.[6] I ate everything I wanted. I paid Ernie all my money for food.

"I'll keep this in trust[7] for you, Mary," Ernie said. "Someday you may need five dollars."

I enjoyed every minute with Ernie. He taught me to cook, and I told him Kaw stories.

But Ta-Na-E-Ka was over. As I neared home, I worried. My feet were hardly cut. I hadn't lost a pound. My hair was combed.

My grandfather met me wearing his grandfather's beaded deerskin shirt. "Welcome back," he said in Kaw.

---

6. **the Missouri** (mu ZUHR ee): U.S. river.
7. **in trust**: safe.

I hugged my parents. Then I saw Roger stretched out on the couch. His eyes were red. He'd lost weight. His feet were bloody and sore.

"I made it. I'm a warrior," Roger said.

My grandfather saw I was clean, well fed, and healthy. Finally he asked, "What did you eat to keep you so well?"

"Hamburgers and milkshakes."

"Hamburgers!" my grandfather shouted.

"Milkshakes!" Roger said.

"You didn't say we *had* to eat grasshoppers," I said.

"Tell us all about your Ta-Na-E-Ka," my grandfather ordered.

I told them the whole story.

"That's not what I trained you for," my grandfather said.

"Grandfather, I learned that Ta-Na-E-Ka is important. I handled it my way. And I learned I had nothing to fear. There's no reason in 1947 to eat grasshoppers. Grandfather, I'll bet you never ate one of those rotten berries."

Grandfather laughed aloud! Grandfather never laughed. Never.

"Those berries are terrible," Grandfather said. "I found a dead deer on the first day of my Ta-Na-E-Ka. The deer kept my belly full." Grandfather stopped laughing. "We should send you out again," he said.

Grandfather called me to him. "You should have done what your cousin did. But you know more about what is happening to our people today than I do. You would have passed the test in any time. You can make do in a world that wasn't made for Indians. I don't think you'll have trouble getting along."

Grandfather wasn't entirely right. But I'll tell about that another time.

Your TURN

CONFLICT

Mary might have made several people angry because of how she did her Ta-Na-E-Ka. Who might be angry with her in lines 91–99?

_____
_____
_____
_____

Here's HOW

COMPARE AND CONTRAST

In lines 108–117, I found out that Grandfather didn't really follow the rules of Ta-Na-E-Ka! But he, like Mary, learned how to survive.

TA-NA-E-KA 35

Ta-Na-E-Ka

Conflict Chart

Conflicts happen when characters struggle against other characters. Characters might also struggle against outside forces or themselves. In "Ta-Na-E-Ka," Mary faces conflicts with several people. Fill out the chart below to better understand Mary's conflicts.

First, describe Mary's conflict with her grandfather. Then, describe her conflicts with Roger, Mrs. Richardson, and Ernie. One box has been filled in for you.

Mary's conflict with her grandfather
_____
_____

Mary's conflict with Roger, her cousin
_____
_____

Mary's conflict with Mrs. Richardson, her teacher
Mary expects Mrs. Richardson to agree with her. Mrs. Richardson doesn't. She says Mary is looking down on her roots. She thinks Mary should have more respect for her family's traditions.

Mary's conflict with Ernie, the restaurant owner
_____
_____

Ta-Na-E-Ka

Vocabulary

A. Match the words below with their definitions. Write the letter of the correct definition next to each word. One has been done for you.

Word Bank
accountant
roots
reservation
in trust
rituals

_____ 1. accountant   a. traditional ceremonies

__e__ 2. roots   b. held safely

_____ 3. reservation   c. a person who keeps money records

_____ 4. in trust   d. place where some American Indians live

_____ 5. rituals   e. ancestors and their culture and history

B. Answer the following questions. One has been done for you.

1. Why do you think we need <u>accountants</u>?
   _____

2. Why might a family think that its <u>roots</u> are important?
   _____

3. When you make a <u>reservation</u> at a restaurant, the restaurant will hold a table until you get there. How is this different from the <u>reservation</u> in "Ta-Na-E-Ka"?
   _____

4. How is the meaning of <u>in trust</u> similar to the meaning of *trust*?
   <u>When you "trust" someone, you think they're honest. Honest people will hold</u>
   <u>things safely.</u>

TA-NA-E-KA 37

The Wind People

Reading Skill: Outlining

Outlining is a way to take notes about informational texts. An outline includes the most important ideas, or **main ideas,** in a section of a selection. A main idea is not always stated. Sometimes you have to figure out the main idea by looking at all the details in a paragraph or section.

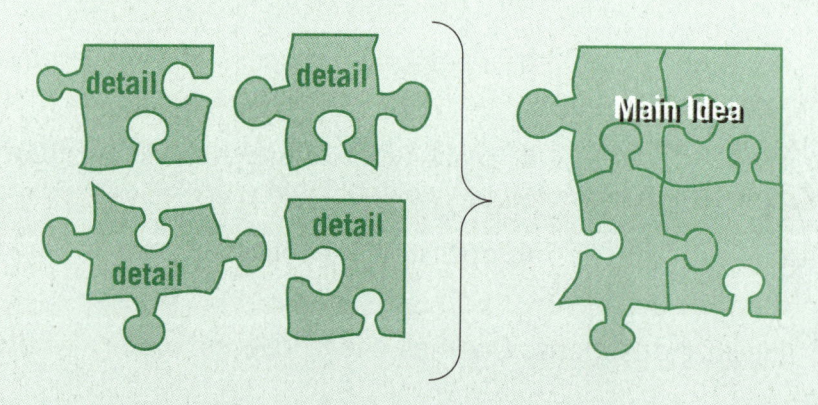

Each part of a story, article, or essay may have a main idea. Every time you finish a section of the article that seems to have a main idea, you can add to your outline. In addition to the main ideas, an outline usually includes the important details that support each main idea.

I. Main idea
    A. First detail supporting main idea #1
    B. Second detail supporting main idea #1

Into the History Article

The "Wind People" is another name for the Kaw, an American Indian people. The last member of the Kaw died in 2000. Today, the Kaw live on through stories like "Ta-Na-E-Ka."

The Wind People

Based on the History Article by
Flo Ota De Lange

Here's HOW

OUTLINING

This piece of writing has three main sections. The first section tells the Kaws' story of how they came to be. The Kaw needed more space, and the Great Spirit gave it to them. That's the first idea: The Kaw were given room to grow.

Your TURN

OUTLINING

Re-read the second section, "European Arrivals." In lines 17–19, underline the things that changed for the Kaw when the Europeans came.

Your TURN

OUTLINING

Re-read the third section, "The End of the Kaw." Then, write down the main idea of that section on the following lines.

_____
_____
_____
_____

The Kaw Creation Myth

A Kaw story explains how the world came into being: Many years ago their people lived on an island too small for them. The Kaw mothers begged the Great Spirit for more
5   space. The Great Spirit sent beavers and turtles to make the island bigger. They shaped the land using materials from the bottom of the great waters. The Kaw people now had room to grow.

European Arrivals

10   By the early 1800s, the Kaw nation stretched over twenty million acres. Then French explorers arrived. They wanted to learn the names of the new rivers and mountains.

But the French wrote down these names in their own language. Sometimes the Kaw sounds did not exist in
15   French. This is how *U-Moln-Holn* became *Omaha* and *Wi-Tsi-Ta* became *Wichita*.

Soon, European immigrants[1] wanted to live on Kaw land. The immigrants brought deadly diseases such as smallpox.[2] Many Kaw people died from these diseases.

The End of the Kaw

In 1825, the U.S. government opened Kaw land to other peoples. The Kaw themselves were confined to two million acres of what is now Kansas. In 1872, the government moved the nation to a 100,000-acre reservation[3] in
25   Oklahoma. This move made the Kaw very weak.

By 1995, only four Kaw were left: William Mehojah, his brother, and two nephews. Mr. Mehojah's last nephew died in 1998. By the year 2000, the Kaw were gone forever.

---

1. **immigrants:** people who leave their nation to live in another nation.
2. **smallpox:** deadly virus that causes pitted scars, fevers, and vomiting.
3. **reservation:** land set aside for American Indian tribes; land belonging to them.

Outline Organizer

In the organizer below, outline "The Wind People." You can use your responses to the Your Turns on page 40. Lines 1–8 of the article have been outlined for you. NOTE: In formal outlines, the main ideas are identified by roman numerals (I, II, III) instead of Arabic numbers (1, 2, 3).

Main Idea I:

1. The Kaw had a creation story

    Supporting Detail:

    A. The Kaw lived on an island that was too small.

    Supporting Detail:

    B. Because of this, Kaw mothers prayed to the Great Spirit.

    Supporting Detail:

    C. As a result, beavers, and turtles came to enlarge the island. Soon it was large enough for the Kaw people.

Main Idea II:
_____
_____

Supporting Details:
_____
_____

Main Idea III:
_____
_____

Supporting Details:
_____
_____

Before You Read

The Bracelet

Literary Focus: First-Person Point of View

A story's **point of view** depends on who the narrator is. Often a character inside the story narrates, or tells, it. In that case, the story is told from the **first-person point of view.** The narrator uses *I* and *me* when telling the story.

"The Bracelet" is told from the first-person point of view. That means we know only what the narrator, Ruri, tells us. We may find out a lot about Ruri's feelings. But we won't be sure what other characters think or feel.

Reading Skill: Making Predictions

As you read "The Bracelet," questions in the margin will ask you to guess what will happen next. But don't just make wild guesses. Instead, use

- clues from the text
- your own knowledge, like your knowledge of how people are

Guessing in this way is called **making predictions.** As you read on, check to see if your predictions were right.

Into the Short Story

Japan and the United States were at war in 1942. The U.S. government was afraid Japanese people living in the United States were spies. Thousands of Japanese Americans were forced to go to faraway camps. There, they lived in cramped, cheap housing. Soldiers guarded them.

The Bracelet

Based on the Story by
Yoshiko Uchida

Here's HOW

VOCABULARY

My teacher told me about Pearl Harbor, mentioned in line 13. It is a naval base in Hawaii. On December 7, 1941, Japanese planes bombed U.S. battleships in Pearl Harbor. Many Americans were killed. This tragedy caused the United States to enter World War II.

Here's HOW

MAKING PREDICTIONS

I can tell from lines 3 and 19 that Ruri's mother is sad and Laurie is sad. It looks like something bad is about to happen.

---

1 "Mama, is it time to go?"

"It's almost time, Ruri," my mother said. I had never seen her face so sad.

I looked at my empty room and the empty house. It was like a gift box after the nice thing inside was gone, just a lot of nothing.

It was April 21, 1942. The United States and Japan were at war. The government was sending all Japanese on the West Coast to internment camps.[1]

10 The doorbell rang. I hoped there would be a message from Papa. He was in a camp in Montana. The FBI had picked up Papa and hundreds of other Japanese community leaders on the very day Japan bombed Pearl Harbor. The government thought Japanese people were dangerous

15 enemies now. But Papa was no more dangerous than the mayor of our city, and he was just as loyal. He had lived here since 1917.

I opened the door and saw my best friend, Laurie. She held a present. Her face drooped like a wilted[2] tulip.

20 "Hi," she said. "I came to say good-bye." She handed me the gift. "It's a bracelet," she said. "Put it on so you won't have to pack it." She knew I didn't have one inch of space left in my suitcase. Mama told us that we could take only two suitcases each.

25 Laurie helped me put on the bracelet before she left. It was a thin gold chain with a heart hanging from it. I promised to wear the bracelet always.

"Well, goodbye then," Laurie said. "Come home soon."

---

1. **internment** (ihn TURN mihnt) **camps:** camps where people were kept together and not allowed to leave.
2. **wilted** (WIHLT ehd): became limp, like a flower without water.

"The Bracelet" by Yoshiko Uchida adapted from *The Scribner Anthology for Young People*, edited by Anne Diven. Copyright © 1976 by Yoshiko Uchida. Retold by Holt, Rinehart and Winston. Reproduced by permission of **Atheneum Books for Young Readers**, an imprint of Simon & Schuster Children's Publishing Division.

"I will," I said. I did not know if I would ever return.

30 I watched Laurie go down the block. Her blond pigtails bounced as she walked. I wondered who would sit at my desk at school now that I was gone. Laurie kept turning and waving until she got to the corner. I didn't want to watch anymore. I slammed the door shut.

35 Mrs. Simpson, our other neighbor, came to the door next. She was there to drive us to a church. There we would get on a bus.

I picked up my two suitcases. Each one had a tag with my name and our family number on it. Every Japanese family 40 had to register. We were Family Number 13453.

Mama went from room to room. In her mind, she seemed to be taking pictures of the house.

She took a long last look at Papa's garden. The irises[3] beside the fish pond were blooming. Papa had always cut the 45 first iris blossom for Mama. Now the garden looked the way I felt. Empty and lonely.

When Mrs. Simpson dropped us off at the church, I felt even worse. Over a thousand Japanese people were at the church. Some were old; some were young. Some were talking 50 and laughing. Others were crying. No one knew exactly what was going to happen to us. We knew only that we were headed to the Tanforan Racetracks.[4] The area was now a camp for the Japanese. Fourteen other camps like ours were along the West Coast.

55 The soldiers standing at the doorway scared me. They were carrying guns. I wondered if they thought we would try to run away. If we did, would they shoot us?

A long line of buses waited to take us to camp. I sat with my sister Keiko, and Mama sat behind us. The bus passed the

---

3. **irises** (Y rihs uhz): plants with big, showy flowers.
4. **Tanforan** (TAN fuh RAN) **Racetracks**: horse-racing track located south of San Francisco. It burned down in 1964.

Here's HOW
VOCABULARY

I recognize the word *register* in line 40. I remember last year my father took me to register for summer camp. I registered by writing down my name, phone number, and address on a card. Then I gave the card to a camp worker.

Here's HOW
FIRST-PERSON POINT OF VIEW

I wonder how this story would be different if the mother were telling it. I wonder if she thinks about her husband when she sees the irises. Maybe she's wondering who will feed the fish.

THE BRACELET 45

MAKING PREDICTIONS

Lines 76–80: Do you think Ruri's apartment will be like her piano teacher's apartment? Explain.

_____
_____
_____

FIRST-PERSON POINT OF VIEW

Re-read lines 81–86. Then think about how the mother might be feeling at this moment. On the lines below, write four or five descriptive words that she might use to show her feelings about the family's "apartment."

_____
_____
_____

---

60 small Japanese food store where Mama used to shop. The windows were boarded up, but a sign on the door read, "We are loyal Americans."

We were all loyal Americans. Most of us were citizens because we had been born here. But our parents, who had 65 come from Japan, couldn't become citizens. A law kept Asians from becoming citizens. Now everybody with a Japanese face would be shipped off to camps.

"It's silly," Keiko said. "Any Japanese spies would have gone back to Japan long ago."

70 "I'll say," I agreed. My sister was in high school and she ought to know, I thought.

Armed guards stood at the gate of Tanforan. Barbed wire circled the grounds. I felt I was entering a prison. In a huge room, doctors checked us for diseases. We were told we 75 would live in Barrack 16, Apartment 40.

"Mama!" I said. "We're going to live in an apartment!" My piano teacher lived in an apartment. It was in a huge building in San Francisco. It had an elevator and thick carpets in the halls. A house was all right, but an apartment seemed 80 wonderful.

We came to a long stable[5] that had once held horses. Each stall[6] had a number painted on it. We found Apartment 40. The stall was narrow and dark. There were two small windows on each side of the door. Three folded army cots[7] 85 were on the dusty floor. One light bulb hung from the ceiling. This was our apartment. It still smelled of horses.

"We'll fix it up," Mama began. "I'll make curtains and cushions too, and . . ." She stopped. She could think of no more to say.

---

5. **stable:** a building where horses live.
6. **stall:** a space separated by walls where one horse lives.
7. **cots:** narrow beds that can be folded up.

Mr. Noma, our friend, rushed off to get us mattresses. I think he left so that he wouldn't have to see Mama cry. But Mama didn't cry. She just got a broom and swept. "Will you girls set up the cots?" she asked.

After we'd put up the last cot, I saw my bracelet was gone. "I've lost Laurie's bracelet!" I screamed. "My bracelet's gone!"

We looked everywhere. I thought of my promise to Laurie. I wasn't ever going to take the bracelet off. And I had lost it on my very first day in camp. I wanted to cry.

I looked for it all the time we were at the camp. I didn't stop until we were sent to another camp in Utah.

But Mama said I didn't need a bracelet to remember Laurie. And I didn't need anything to remember Papa or our home. Or everyone and everything we loved and had left behind.

"Those are things we can carry in our hearts. We take them with us everywhere," she said.

I guess she was right. I've never forgotten Laurie, even now.

Your TURN

FIRST-PERSON POINT OF VIEW

Imagine Laurie found out that Ruri had just lost the bracelet. What do you think Laurie would say to Ruri at that moment? Write down Laurie's response.

Your TURN

MAKING PREDICTIONS

Do you think that Ruri will see Laurie again? What makes you say so?

The Bracelet

Point-of-View Chart

When we read a story told from the first-person point of view, we get a look into the mind of one character. But that's only part of the story. It can be fun to imagine how other characters might think and feel. The left-hand column of the chart below contains Ruri's descriptions of three scenes. In the right-hand column, rewrite each scene from the point of view of another character in the story. The first scene has been done for you.

Ruri's Point of View	Another Point of View
"I watched Laurie go down the block. Her blond pigtails bounced as she walked. I wondered who would sit at my desk at school now that I was gone. Laurie kept turning and waving until she got to the corner. I didn't want to watch anymore. I slammed the door shut." (lines 30–34)	**Laurie's point of view:** I didn't know what to say anymore, so I turned away. I had in my mind a picture of Ruri's thin, graceful wrist wearing the bracelet. I wondered who would play dress-up with me now that she was gone. I didn't think I would play dress-up anymore anyway. I suddenly felt older. Then I heard the door slam, and I felt like crying.
"She took a long last look at Papa's garden. The irises beside the fish pond were blooming. Papa had always cut the first iris blossom for Mama. Now the garden looked the way I felt. Empty and lonely." (lines 43–46)	**Mama's point of view:**
"The soldiers standing at the doorway scared me. They were carrying guns. I wondered if they thought we would try to run away. If we did, would they shoot us?" (Lines 55–57)	**A soldier's point of view:**

The Bracelet

Vocabulary

A. Match words and definitions. Write the letter of the correct definition next to each word. One has been completed for you.

Word Bank
internment
wilt
stable
stall
cots

__c__ 1. internment   **a.** a building where horses live

_____ 2. wilted   **b.** became limp from lack of water or too much heat

_____ 3. stable   **c.** being kept from leaving

_____ 4. stall   **d.** narrow beds that can be folded up

_____ 5. cots   **e.** a space separated by walls where one horse lives

B. Choose three words from the Word Bank. Use each word in a sentence of your own.

1. _____
   _____

2. _____
   _____

3. _____
   _____

Before You Read

Wartime Mistakes, Peacetime Apologies

Reading Skill: Taking Notes

How do you keep track of what you read? You take notes! One way to take notes is to find important dates in what you read. This way works well when you read about history. Dates matter in history.

- When did World War II start?
- When did the United States enter the war?
- When did the war finally end?

These are the kinds of questions you answer in history class. When you see a date, pay attention. Something important probably happened on the date.

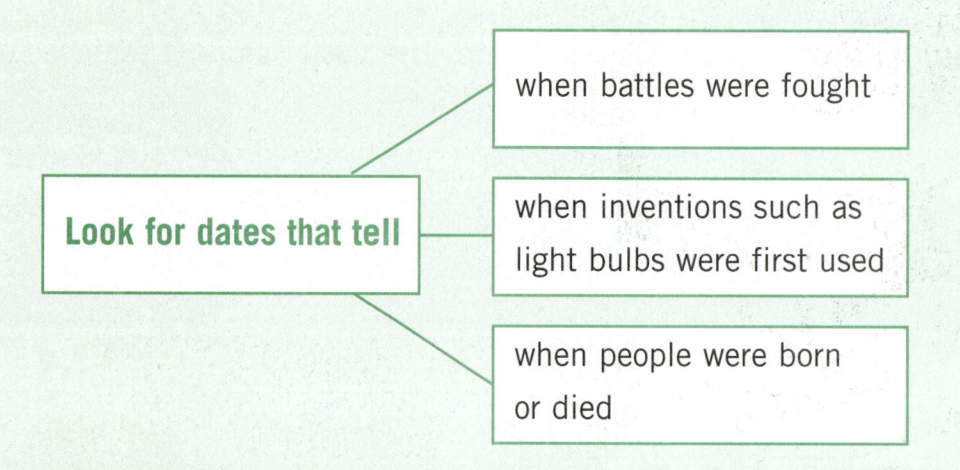

Look for dates that tell
- when battles were fought
- when inventions such as light bulbs were first used
- when people were born or died

Into the Article

From 1942 to 1945, Japanese Americans were treated badly. The United States was at war with Japan. The president and other Americans didn't trust Japanese Americans, even though many of these people had lived in the United States a long time. Japanese Americans lost their homes and jobs. Later, the United States realized it had made a mistake and said it was sorry.

Wartime Mistakes, Peacetime Apologies

Based on the Article by **Nancy Day**

Here's HOW

TAKING NOTES

Right away, I see a date—December 7, 1941. I've circled the date. Now I'll write what happened: Japan attacked the United States.

Your TURN

TAKING NOTES

Dates stand out from the words on the page. Circle three other dates on this page. Then, answer the questions below.

What happened in 1942?

_____
_____
_____
_____

What happened in 1945?

_____
_____
_____
_____

What happened in 1990?

_____
_____
_____
_____

---

1   **O**n December 7, 1941, Japan attacked the United States. Then in 1942, President Roosevelt signed a war order.[1] It changed many lives. The order put Japanese Americans in camps. The camps were like prisons.

5   A teacher named Yoshiko Imamoto had lived in America for twenty-four years. In March 1942, three lawmen came to her home. They let her pack a nightgown and a Bible. Then, they took her to jail.

The war ended in 1945. Japanese Americans had to
10 start over. They had lost their jobs and their homes. They felt hurt. They had been good citizens. The United States had treated them badly. They wanted America to say it had been wrong. They wanted payment for their pain.

Many years later, the government decided the order
15 had been unjust.[2] All citizens have the same rights. Our country should not have put citizens in camps. Each camp survivor should receive twenty thousand dollars. America should say it was sorry.

Some people said that no one should be paid. The order had
20 been correct. The government had to protect everyone.

Some Japanese Americans had not obeyed the war orders. They went to jail. Three of them sued[3] the country and won their case. The court said the Japanese Americans had done nothing wrong. They had the same rights as other Americans.

25 In 1990, at age ninety-three, Imamoto received a twenty-thousand dollar check and a note. Almost fifty years had passed. And America had finally paid for its mistake. America had apologized.

---

1. **order:** a rule or law that must be obeyed.
2. **unjust** (uhn JUHST): not fair.
3. **sued** (sood): brought to a court of law to seek justice or gain a right.

"Wartime Mistakes, Peacetime Apologies" by Nancy Day Sakaduski adapted from *Cobblestone: Japanese Americans*, April 1996. Copyright © 1996 by Cobblestone Publishing Company. Retold by Holt, Rinehart and Winston. All rights reserved. Reproduced by permission of **Cobblestone Publishing Company, 30 Grove Street, Suite C, Peterborough, NH 03458, a division of Carus Publishing Company.**

Taking Notes

Taking notes will help you remember what you read. How do you take good notes? One way is to keep track of dates. When a date shows up in a history article, you get a clue that something important happened.

Time Line

A **time line** is a kind of chart that shows events in time order. In a time line, important events are listed from beginning to end. Fill out this time line with events from "Wartime Mistakes, Peacetime Apologies." One of the events has been written for you.

1941	1942	1945	1990
	• President Roosevelt signs an order to make all Japanese Americans move to camps.		

Wartime Mistakes, Peacetime Apologies 53

Everybody Is Different, but the Same Too

Reading Skill: Evaluating Conclusions

A writer's **conclusion** is an idea that the writer comes up with based on evidence. Conclusions are usually opinions, not proven facts. Your job as a reader is to evaluate the writer's conclusions. To do that, **summarize** the author's writing. It's like adding numbers: 2 + 2 = 4—not 3, and not 5.

Read the text in the box:

> Have you ever been the "new kid"? It's not easy. You don't know any names. You're not sure how to find your classrooms. You wonder, "Will I make new friends?" Everyone has friends already. Will you fit in?

Now, read this summary statement of the text:

> Being the "new kid" at school can be scary.

This statement "sums up" all seven sentences of the text.

When you read the following interview, identify the writer's conclusion—it's stated at the end. Then, state your own summary of the writing. If your statement is different from the writer's conclusion, the writer's conclusion may be weak or simply wrong.

Into the Interview

In interviews, people answer questions about themselves. This interview comes from a book called *Newcomers to America.* It's about being the "new kid." Find out what one student, Nilou, says about "fitting in" in a new place.

Everybody Is Different, but the Same Too

FROM Newcomers to America

Based on the Interview with **Nilou**

Here's HOW

EVALUATING CONCLUSIONS

If I stop to summarize each paragraph, I can remember it. So, how would I sum up the first few lines? "Special holidays and special ways of doing things keep culture alive." Later, I'll see if this supports the writer's conclusion.

Your TURN

EVALUATING CONCLUSIONS

Lines 17–22 make an important point. Re-read these lines. Then, write your summary of them.

_____
_____
_____
_____

Your TURN

EVALUATING CONCLUSIONS

In lines 27–29, which sentence is Nilou's overall conclusion? Underline it.

---

1 Keeping a culture alive is hard. I think I am partly Iranian, partly American. We keep our old ways alive by traditions and by the five holidays we celebrate.

In Iran, as a woman, I would go to school. However,
5 colleges are very hard to get into. In Iran I would have to get a job after high school. I would have to get married when I'm twenty or something. Most women don't work in high positions.[1] I'm happy to be here.

In school there is a Spanish club and a Chinese club.
10 We are trying to make an Iranian club. I don't know if it will work. There are only about eleven or twelve kids.

I think a club is a way of trying to keep the culture alive. In the Hispanic club, every Thursday, they get together and they dance. We also have an international concert that we
15 can go to. You can sing if you like, dance, bring food, you know, just whatever you want to do to present your culture.

When I came to public school, I saw that America is really a melting pot.[2] America borrows many things from other cultures. So there is no American way. You can't look
20 at people and say they look like Americans. Everybody is American. That was when I realized I am American— because all Americans are different.

We should teach that people are people and everybody is the same. They just have different ways of handling
25 problems and different lifestyles. We probably have the same goals.

My friends are from all different parts of the world. My American friends are different. My Iranian friends are different. Everybody is different, but the same too.

---

1. **positions:** jobs.
2. **melting pot:** place where people from many nations live together.

"Nilou" adapted from *Newcomers to America: Stories of Today's Young Immigrants* by Judith E. Greenberg. Copyright © 1996 by Judith E. Greenberg. Retold by Holt, Rinehart and Winston. Reproduced by permission of **Grolier Publishing Company, a division of Scholastic Inc.**

Evaluating Conclusions Chart

The writer's **conclusion** is the idea he or she forms about a set of evidence. A reader's job is to **evaluate,** or judge, writers' conclusions. In the chart below, summarize each paragraph. For some, use your responses to Your Turns on page 56. Others have been done for you. Then, answer the question the follows.

Evaluation Chart

Paragraph Number	Summary of Paragraph
Paragraph 1 (lines 1–3)	Special holidays and special ways of doing things keep culture alive.
Paragraph 2 (lines 4–8)	
Paragraph 3 (lines 9–11)	
Paragraph 4 (lines 12–16)	Clubs and the international concert are two ways students' cultures are kept alive at school.
Paragraph 5 (lines 17–22)	
Paragraph 6 (lines 23–26)	Although people have different lifestyles and approaches to problems, all people have the same goals, and this makes all people the same.
Paragraph 7—State the writer's conclusion (lines 27–29):	

Now evaluate the writer's conclusion. Look at each summary statement in the chart. Do you agree that these statements "add up" to the writer's conclusion? Why or why not?

_____

_____

_____

Before You Read

The Emperor's New Clothes

Literary Focus: Theme

Theme is a story's message about life. You can usually say the theme in one sentence. For example, the theme in "The Three Little Pigs" is "Quality and hard work pay off." As you read, see what message you get from the following story.

Reading Skill: Making Generalizations

A **generalization** is an overall idea supported by several examples or facts. Generalizations usually contain words like *most, many,* or *usually*. That's because we make generalizations from a few facts or examples. Other facts or examples may not support the generalization.

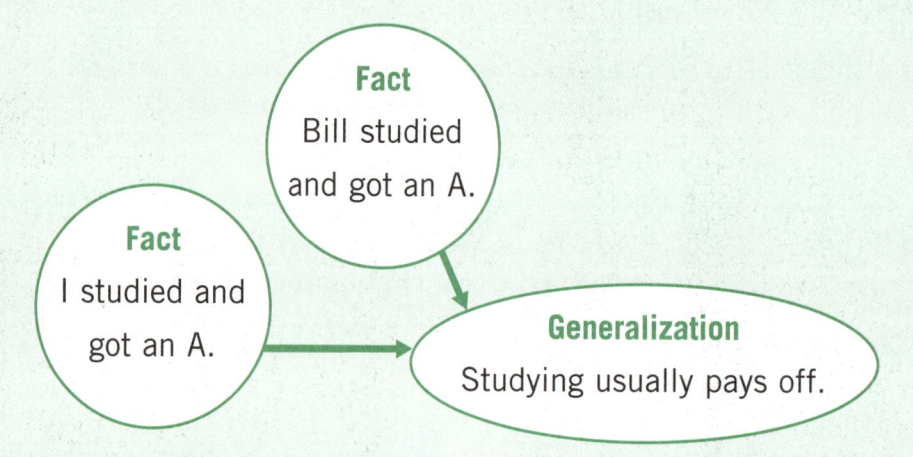

Fact
Bill studied and got an A.

Fact
I studied and got an A.

Generalization
Studying usually pays off.

Into the Story

"The Emperor's New Clothes" is a fairy tale. The theme of a fairy tale often teaches a lesson. Like many fairy tales, this one is about an Emperor who rules a large country. In this tale, two crooks pretend to weave a magical cloth. The Emperor decides he needs clothes made out of this cloth. Read about the Emperor and his new clothes. What lesson can this story teach you?

THE EMPEROR'S NEW CLOTHES

Based on the Fairy Tale by
Hans Christian Andersen

Here's HOW

MAKING GENERALIZATIONS

The Emperor seems too concerned about how he looks. He also doesn't want to appear foolish. In general, the Emperor is too proud. I underlined examples in the story that support my generalization.

Here's HOW

THEME

I know that in real life some people will do anything to avoid looking foolish. I circled the sentences in lines 29-31 that show this theme in the story.

Many years ago there lived an Emperor who spent all his money on new clothes. He did not care for his soldiers, or for driving in the woods. All he wanted was to show off his new clothes to the people in his empire.

One day two crooks came to the city where the Emperor lived. They said that they could weave a cloth that had beautiful colors and patterns. Not only was their cloth beautiful, but the clothes made of this material were invisible to any man who was not worthy of his job, or who was hopelessly stupid.

The Emperor thought, "If I wore these clothes made from this cloth, I would know which men are unfit for their jobs and which are stupid. I must have this cloth woven for me right away." So he gave a lot of money to the two crooks and told them to begin work at once.

The two crooks set up two empty looms[1] and pretended to weave. They asked for the finest silk and the most precious gold, which they put into their own bags.

Everybody in the town knew about the wonderful cloth. All the people wanted to find out how bad or stupid their neighbors were.

The Emperor knew he would be able to see the cloth. However, he thought he would send somebody else first to see how things were going.

He sent his most honest official to where the two crooks sat working at the empty looms. The crooks asked the official to step closer and admire the cloth.

The poor man opened his eyes wide, but he could see nothing. He thought, "Can I be so stupid? Nobody must know! I must not tell anyone that I cannot see the cloth. I shall tell the Emperor that I am very pleased with it."

---

1. **looms:** special machines for weaving thread into cloth.

Now the two crooks asked for more money, more silk, and more gold, which they kept all for themselves.

The Emperor sent another honest official to see if the cloth was nearly finished. Like the first official, he looked but could see nothing.

"I am not stupid," thought the man, "so it must be that I am unfit for my job. I must not let anyone know it." So he told the Emperor that the cloth was beautiful.

At last the Emperor went to see the cloth for himself.

"Is it not magnificent?" said the crooks, pointing to the empty looms.

"What is this?" thought the Emperor. "I do not see anything at all. Am I stupid? Am I unfit to be Emperor? That would be the most dreadful[2] thing that could happen to me!"

"Yes, it is very beautiful," said the Emperor. "It has my highest approval."

It was decided that the crooks would sew magnificent new clothes from the wonderful cloth. The Emperor would wear the new clothes at a great procession[3] that was soon to take place.

The crooks pretended to take the cloth from the loom. They snipped the air with big scissors. They sewed with needles without any thread. And at last they said, "Now the Emperor's new clothes are ready!"

The Emperor, followed by all his noblest[4] attendants, arrived. The Emperor took off all his clothes, and the crooks pretended to put the new clothes on him, including the robe. Then, the Emperor looked at himself in the mirror. "Don't my new clothes fit me beautifully?" he said, turning this way and that before the mirror so that everyone would think he was admiring his clothes.

---

2. **dreadful** (DREHD ful): terrible.
3. **procession** (pruh SEHSH uhn): parade of people.
4. **noblest**: most honored; finest.

Your TURN

THEME

One of this story's themes is "people will do anything to avoid looking foolish." Underline the sentences in lines 37–47 that show this theme.

Your TURN

MAKING GENERALIZATIONS

First, re-read lines 40–63. Next, find support for the generalization that the Emperor is too proud. Write down proof for that generalization.

_____
_____
_____
_____
_____
_____
_____
_____

Your Turn

MAKING GENERALIZATIONS

Re-read line 72. What generalization about children can you make from what the child says?

_____
_____
_____
_____
_____
_____

Here's How

VOCABULARY

I wonder what the word *train* means in line 80. Back in lines 64-66, men pretend to carry a "long, trailing robe." I'll bet that's what *train* means. I checked in the dictionary and it means "trailing gown"—I was right!

Then, the procession began, with the Emperor leading the way. Behind him, the men who were to carry the edge of the long, trailing robe pretended to hold something up in their hands. They didn't dare let people know that they could not see anything.

As the Emperor marched by, all that saw him said, "How marvelous the Emperor's new suit is! How well it fits him! What a fine robe he has!" Nobody would admit that he saw nothing, for then he would be unfit for his job or too stupid.

"But he has nothing on at all," said a little child.

"Good heavens! Hear what the innocent child says!" said the father.

Then the people around him whispered to one another, "A little child says he has nothing on at all!"

At last, all the people shouted, "He has nothing on at all!"

The Emperor was worried, for it seemed to him that the child was right. However, he marched on. The attendants behind him held up the train, which was not there at all.

The Emperor's New Clothes

Theme Chart

Theme is the meaning of a story. The author may not tell you the theme. You may have to decide what the theme is. Think about what the main characters do and say. What did they learn? Look at what the story tells you about real life.

To explore theme in "The Emperor's New Clothes," complete the chart below. Fill in the actions of the main characters in the four outside boxes. Then, think about what you learned as you read the story. Does the story have a message about life? Finally, fill in the theme box in the center of the chart. One action has been filled in for you.

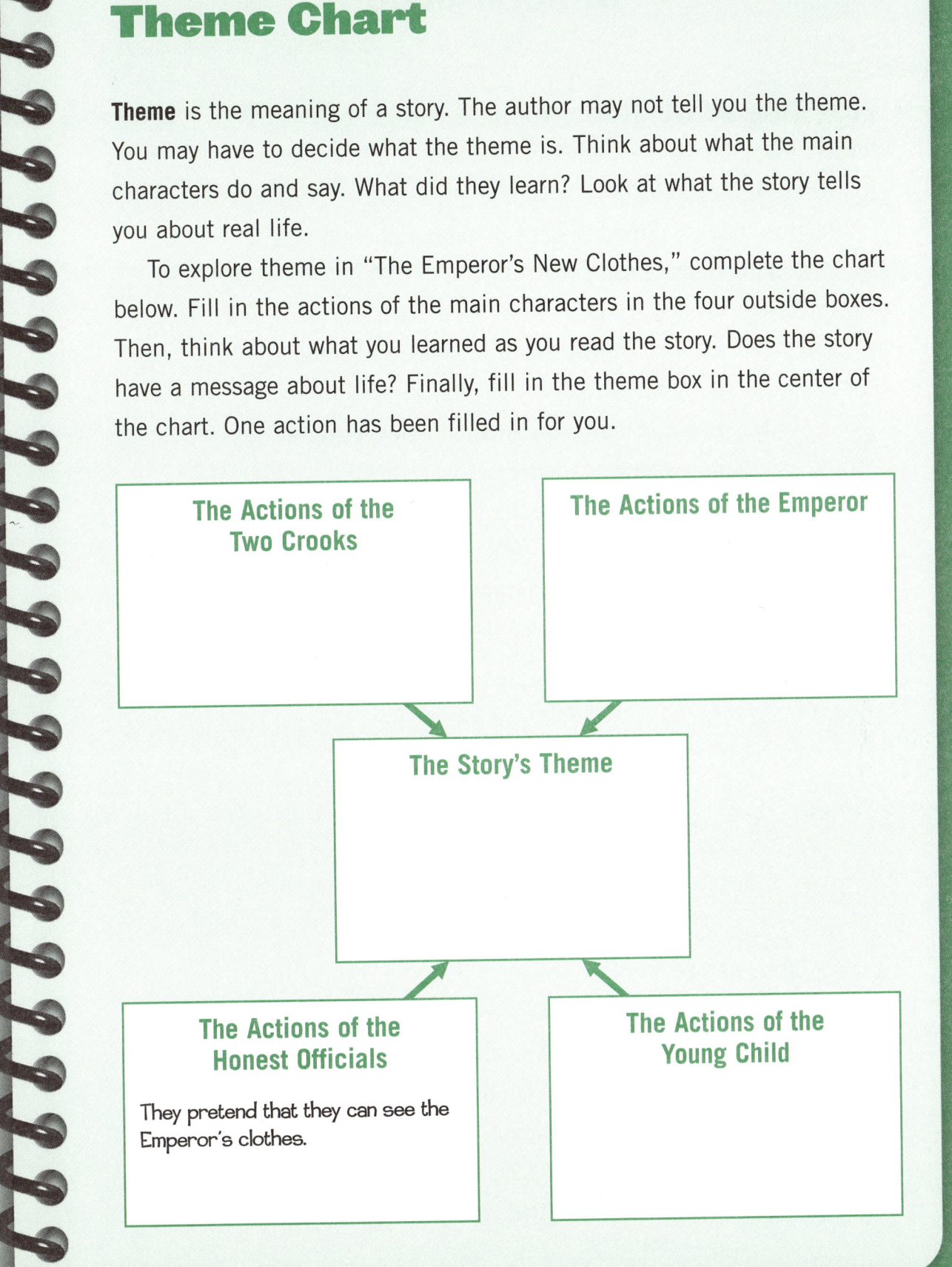

The Actions of the Two Crooks

The Actions of the Emperor

The Story's Theme

The Actions of the Honest Officials

They pretend that they can see the Emperor's clothes.

The Actions of the Young Child

Before You Read

Uniform Style

Reading Skill: Recognizing Evidence

Writers must support their claims. **Evidence** is information that backs up a claim.

Readers look for different kinds of evidence. Here are two important kinds of evidence.

1. A **quotation** is what someone says about a topic. Quotations are easy to spot. They are inside quotation marks:

    "Our school uniforms are blue and gray," says a student at Valley Academy.

2. An **example** makes a claim clearer. It adds a detail about the claim:

    Many students like comfortable clothes. They prefer to wear jeans, t-shirts, and sandals.

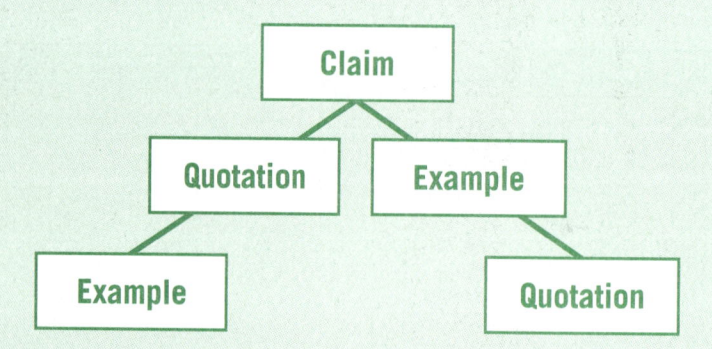

```
              Claim
             /     \
        Quotation   Example
          /             \
      Example         Quotation
```

Into the Article

School uniforms are special clothes just for school. All the girls wear one uniform. All the boys wear another. What do you think about school uniforms? Do they make life easier for students? Or are they just not cool? This article gives reasons to wear uniforms. It also gives reasons not to wear uniforms. See what you think of the evidence.

64 HOLT ADAPTED READER

Uniform Style

Based on the Article by Mara Rockliff

Here's HOW

VOCABULARY

Line 7 says that some teachers *favor* uniforms. The word *favor* can mean "to like something." It can also mean "a helpful action." Which meaning is used here? It must mean that teachers *like* uniforms.

Here's HOW

RECOGNIZING EVIDENCE

I know that a quotation, or what a person says, can support a claim. I can underline Hortencia Llanas's words. They tell why she likes school uniforms.

Your TURN

RECOGNIZING EVIDENCE

Read lines 25–27 again. Can you see two examples of how uniforms make schools safer? Underline both examples.

1   Why are many U.S. public schools considering[1] uniforms? Students wearing uniforms "know they are going to school to learn, not going outside to play," says Mary Marquez. Marquez is a principal in Long Beach, California.
5   Her school requires uniforms.

Kids like to wear clothes that make them feel cool. However, many teachers and principals favor uniforms. They think uniforms make kids behave and be better students.

What about the right for students to express themselves?
10 That's what concerns[2] many students and parents. Some have even sued[3] schools that make students wear uniforms.

Other parents are tired of bills for their children's clothes. They are glad uniforms keep costs down. Many students also welcome an end to the clothing war. "I don't worry about
15 what I wear in the morning," says uniform wearer Hortencia Llanas. "I just slip on the clothes."

People that support uniforms seem to say some crazy things. For instance, how could wearing uniforms keep schools safer? But this claim makes sense. Sometimes
20 students fight over clothing like leather jackets. But nobody can fight over the jackets if they can't be worn at school. And people who don't belong on school grounds won't be wearing uniforms. This will make them stand out among students.
25 In Long Beach, facts tell the story: School crime dropped 36 percent, and fighting dropped 51 percent. These changes happened after students began wearing uniforms.

In public schools across the country, this issue is undecided. But many people ask, "Why not give uniforms
30 a try?"

---

1. **considering** (kuhn SIHD uhr ihng): thinking about.
2. **concerns** (kuhn SURNZ): worries.
3. **sued** (sood): taken to a court of law to seek justice or gain a right.

Recognizing Evidence

One person may write, "School uniforms are a good idea." Another may write, "Students shouldn't have to wear a uniform to school." Which writer do you believe? Well, that might depend on how the writers support their claims. Both writers must support their claims with evidence. **Evidence** is information that backs up a claim.

Evidence Chart

The writer of "Uniform Style" likes school uniforms. She thinks uniforms help students. She gives evidence for her claims.

Read the first sentence in the Evidence Box. Decide if it supports Claim 1 or Claim 2, and write it under that claim. Do the same for each evidence statement. One has been done for you.

Evidence Box
Students don't have to choose clothes every morning.
Students don't fight over clothing.
Students know school time is for learning, not for playing.
~~Parents don't have to spend so much money on clothes.~~
School crime drops when students wear uniforms.

Claim 1: Uniforms make life easier for students and their parents.	**Claim 2:** Uniforms make schools safer.
1.	1.
2.	2.
3. Parents don't have to spend so much money on clothes.	3.

Before You Read

Baucis and Philemon

Literary Focus: Universal Themes

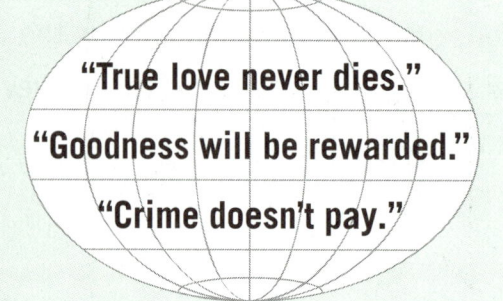

"True love never dies."

"Goodness will be rewarded."

"Crime doesn't pay."

Do these sayings sound familiar? You have probably heard a story or seen a movie where one of these sayings was the **theme,** or message. Some themes, like those above, are **universal.** They appear in stories from different time periods and different parts of the world.

Reading Skill: Recognizing Connections

When you read, it helps to **recognize connections.** When you read a myth, like "Baucis and Philemon," you may find lots of connections — connections to books and movies, even to your own values. That's because many myths are universal. They express values shared by people around the world.

Into the Story

In Greek mythology, Zeus (zoos) is the chief god. The god Hermes (HER meez) is the messenger to the other gods. At the beginning of this myth, both gods have undergone a **metamorphosis** (MET uh MOR fuh sis)—a change in shape or form—to become human.

Baucis and Philemon

BASED ON THE MYTH RETOLD BY
Olivia Coolidge

Here's HOW

RECOGNIZING CONNECTIONS

Baucis and Philemon remind me of my grandmother. Whenever anyone goes to her house, she piles food in front of them.

Your TURN

RECOGNIZING CONNECTIONS

Re-read lines 14–15. Does Philemon's experience connect to anything you've read or heard before? If so, what?

_____

_____

_____

Here's HOW

VOCABULARY

Unworthy (line 21) is a combination of the prefix *un-* and the word *worthy*. *Worthy* means "worth something." *Un-* makes a word mean the opposite. So *unworthy* must mean "not worth something." I've underlined this word.

One time Zeus and Hermes visited the earth in human form. They traveled from door to door seeking food and shelter. Everyone refused them except for a poor old couple named Baucis[1] and Philemon.[2]

5 Though they had little, they offered their best to the two strangers. They seated their guests on a simple handmade couch. Then they began to set the rickety[3] table. Philemon fetched[4] a cabbage from the garden. He got out some home-cured bacon. Baucis set out her best treats: olives, pickled 10 cherries, cream cheese, baked eggs, and wine.

Philemon wanted to catch and kill their only goose, but the guests begged him not to trouble himself. The old couple kept refilling their guests' bowls. Soon a week's worth of food was eaten. Philemon went to refill the wine bowl. To his 15 amazement, it refilled itself. He knew then that their guests were not men but gods.

Hermes said, "You have shown us great kindness this day. Those who have refused us will be punished. You, however, shall be rewarded. Tell us what you will have."

20 Philemon replied, "We have never turned away a stranger. But to serve the gods is a great honor unworthy of this humble[5] cottage. Please turn it into a temple. Then we may worship the gods here all the rest of our days."

"But is there nothing you want for yourselves?" asked 25 Hermes.

The old man glanced at his dear old wife. Then he said, "Our companionship has been the source of our joy in good

---

1. **Baucis** (BAW sis).
2. **Philemon** (fih LEE muhn).
3. **rickety** (RIHK iht ee): likely to break because of weak construction; shaky.
4. **fetched** (fehcht): went and got.
5. **humble** (HUHM bl): low in rank; simple, undecorated.

"Baucis and Philemon" adapted from *Greek Myths* by Olivia Coolidge. Copyright © 1949 and renewed ©1977 by Olivia E. Coolidge. All rights reserved. Retold by Holt, Rinehart and Winston. Reproduced by permission of **Houghton Mifflin Company**.

times and the source of our comfort in bad times. Let us die in the same hour so that neither of us will be left without the other."

Baucis nodded in agreement.

Hermes approved. "You shall have your wish," he said.

So the humble cottage became a temple. Baucis and Philemon became its priestess and priest. Neighbors came to worship and left offerings to aid the old couple.

Baucis and Philemon lived happily. They became so old they seemed to be able to move only by clutching onto each other. One evening they shuffled together to the end of the temple path. There they turned to admire the beautiful temple. As they stood, they felt themselves stiffen and change. Each said "Farewell" to the other before disappearing. In their place stood two trees growing side by side with branches intertwined. They seemed to nod and whisper to each other in the breeze.

VOCABULARY

What does *offerings* mean in line 35? Some clues have been underlined to help you guess.

Here's HOW

UNIVERSAL THEMES

Philemon wishes that he and Baucis will die at the same moment. Zeus and Hermes make sure that, in a way, Baucis and Philemon are together for eternity.

Your TURN

UNIVERSAL THEMES

What themes are expressed by the events around Baucis and Philemon's deaths?

Baucis and Philemon

Universal Themes

A theme is a story's message about life. Myths like "Baucis and Philemon" have been told for so long because they have universal themes. Their messages appeal to people through the ages and around the world.

Recognizing Connections to Universal Themes

Below are some of the themes you can find in "Baucis and Philemon." On the first blank line (a), tell how the theme is shown in the myth. On the second blank line (b), try to name another story, song, movie, or TV show where you recognize the same theme. Then explain how the theme was shown there. Finally, try to think of a fourth universal theme in the myth, and complete the box. Use extra paper if necessary.

Theme #1. Generous people are rewarded.

a. Zeus and Hermes reward Baucis and Philemon for their kindness by granting them two wishes.

b. In the story "The Stone" one of the fairy folk grants Maibon a wish for his kindness.

Theme #2. You do not need to be wealthy to be generous.

a. _____

b. _____

Theme #3. Always be kind to strangers. You never know who they really are.

a. _____

b. _____

Theme #4. _____

a. _____

b. _____

Baucis and Philemon

Vocabulary

Match each word in the word bank at right with its correct definition below. Write the matching word on the blank in front of the correct definition. Then, use the word in a sentence of your own. Write your sentence on the blank lines after the definition. The first one has been done for you.

Word Bank
rickety (line 7)
fetched (line 8)
unworthy (line 21)
humble (line 22)
offerings (line 35)

1. _offerings_ gifts made in worship of a god or spirit
   The young man made offerings at the temple of Zeus.

2. _____ low in rank; simple, undecorated

3. _____ weak, due to poor construction; shaky

4. _____ not deserving; worthless

5. _____ went and got

Before You Read

One Child's Labor of Love

Reading Skill: Fact and Opinion

News reports give you **facts** about an event or a person. What is a fact? It is a bit of information that can be proved true. Here is an example: "Kansas is in the middle of the United States." Can you prove this fact? Yes! Look at a map of the country. You will see Kansas, right in the middle.

News reports also tell you **opinions** about an event or a person. Opinions are not the same as facts. Opinions are a person's beliefs. You can't prove them right or wrong. Here is an example: "Math class is more interesting than art class." This is not a fact. One person may believe it, but another might not.

Statements	Fact	Opinion
Mix blue paint and red paint, and you will get purple paint.	✔	
Anna looked better with long hair.		✔
The scientist said there was more smog today than there was yesterday.	✔	

Into the News Report

Have you ever thought, "How can I make a difference?" Maybe you have helped clean up a city park. Maybe you and your family have taken food to a food bank. All around you are problems. This report is about a young man who saw a big problem. Then he did something about the problem. Read to find out how he helped other young people.

One Child's Labor of Love

Based on the News Report
FROM
60 Minutes

Here's HOW

FACTS AND OPINIONS

I remember that news reports answer questions like *why? when? where? who? what?* and *how?* So I think I will find a lot of *facts* in this selection. The facts answer these questions. In the first few lines, I see facts that can be checked.

Your TURN

FACT AND OPINION

What made Craig start Free the Children? Underline the facts in lines 11–16.

Your TURN

FACT AND OPINION

Read the last sentence of the report. Find out what Craig thinks about the children he met. Are his thoughts facts or opinions? Explain your answer below.

_____
_____
_____
_____
_____

---

1   **E**d Bradley is a *60 Minutes* reporter. He met Craig Kielburger when Craig was thirteen years old. Craig had strong feelings about child slavery.

    Now Craig is sixteen and has met important world
5 leaders. He has won the Franklin and Eleanor Roosevelt Medal of Freedom. Bradley recently revisited Craig.

    At thirteen, Craig told Bradley he was shocked to find out that slavery still exists today—slavery of children. Craig started the Free the Children organization. It has five
10 thousand members and branches[1] in twenty-five countries.

    When Craig was twelve, he read about Iqbal Masih in Pakistan. Iqbal's parents sold him when he was only four years old. Iqbal was chained to a rug loom[2] and worked a twelve-hour day. Finally he escaped and joined the battle
15 against child labor.[3] At age twelve, Iqbal was shot dead. Craig promised to keep Iqbal's cause alive.

    Though his parents were against it, Craig traveled to Asia to meet enslaved children.

    Craig says he found child slavery practiced openly. He met
20 an eight-year-old girl taking apart used syringes[4] and needles. She knew nothing about AIDS or other diseases that she might get from the needles.

    Craig told about giving a street child an orange that she shared with friends. He also recalled a child whose friends
25 carried him because he could not walk. Craig thinks that if these children were in positions of power, the world would truly be a different place.

---

1. **branches:** small groups that belong to one large group.
2. **loom:** a machine on which a rug is made.
3. **labor** (LAY buhr): work.
4. **syringes** (suh RIHNJ ehz): tubes that needles pass through.

From "One Child's Labor of Love" adapted from *60 Minutes II,* October 5, 1999. Copyright © 1999 by CBS Inc. Retold by Holt, Rinehart and Winston. Reproduced by permission of **CBS News Archives.**

Fact and Opinion

A **fact** is a statement that can be proved true. Here's an example: "Mix blue paint and red paint, and you will get purple paint." Can you prove this fact? Of course! Get some blue paint and some red paint. When you mix them, you'll have purple paint.

Opinions are not the same as facts. **Opinions** are a person's beliefs. You can't prove them right or wrong. Here's an example: "Anna looked better with long hair." This is not a fact. You can't prove it. And you may disagree. You may like Anna's new short hair.

Facts and Opinions Chart

Here are some statements from the news report you just read. Read each statement. Decide if it is a fact or an opinion. Check the correct box. One sentence has been done for you.

Statements	Fact	Opinion
Craig Keilburger is a nice young man.		
Child slavery still exists in some places.		
Craig has met with important world leaders.	✔	
People who make children work are mean and bad.		
Craig has won the Medal of Freedom award.		

Before You Read

Separate but Never Equal

Reading Skill: Compare and Contrast

Have you ever talked about how two things are alike? You're **comparing** them. And comparing things tells you a lot: "José's party was like a rock concert. It was loud!"

You probably talk about how two things are different, too. You're **contrasting** them. And contrasting things tells you a lot, as well: "Jesse's party was more fun than José's. The food was better."

In reading we **compare and contrast** to better understand what we read.

Use the graphic organizer below to help you compare and contrast your school to the schools described in the following article.

Schools in the Article	How They Are the Same	My School
White students have their own new textbooks. Black students share old textbooks.	My school and the schools in the article have textbooks.	All students have their own textbooks. Textbooks are all pretty new.

Into the Article

Before 1954, African Americans in the South often were set apart from white people. This system was called **segregation**. African Americans were not allowed to use the same schools or restaurants as whites. The laws in some states said this was okay. The laws said that these places had to be "separate but equal." The following article compares life for blacks to life for whites under segregation.

78 HOLT ADAPTED READER

Separate but Never Equal

Based on the Article by Mara Rockliff

Background

Court cases have names. In the court case *Plessy* v. *Ferguson,* a man named Plessy argued against a judge named Ferguson. The *v.* in the case name stands for *versus.* That's a Latin word that means "against." (It's like *vs.* in *Bulldogs vs. Eagles* or *San Diego vs. Atlanta.*)

Homer Plessy was an African American who lived in Louisiana. Louisiana was a state that had "separate but equal" laws. One of these laws said that there had to be separate train cars for blacks and whites. In 1892, Plessy was forced to leave a train car set aside for whites. Plessy went to court. He argued that the law was bad. The judge was John H. Ferguson. He said Plessy was wrong. Then, the case went to the U.S. Supreme Court.

Most of the judges on the Supreme Court said "separate but equal" laws were okay. Plessy lost his case.

But in 1951 another case about "separate but equal" laws went to court. It was called *Brown* v. *Board of Education of Topeka, Kansas.* The Browns lived in Topeka, Kansas, where schools were segregated. Linda Brown went to an all-black elementary school. Her father Oliver thought segregation was bad. He went to court, but he lost.

Soon, Brown went to the U.S. Supreme Court. In 1954, the Court decided Brown was right. Segregated schools were now against the law in the United States. *Brown* v. *Board of Education* is one of the most important cases ever brought to the Supreme Court.

1   When I was a boy, I would go downtown . . . , and I'd see the signs saying "White" and "Colored"[1] on the water fountains. There'd be a beautiful, shining water fountain in one corner of the store marked "White," and in another corner
5   was just a little spigot[2] marked "Colored."

—U.S. Congressman and civil rights[3] leader John Lewis

In 1896, the U.S. Supreme Court ruled that states could pass laws separating people by skin color. The court said things could be divided by skin color, but they must be equal.
10 This "separate but equal" decision would last for more than fifty years.

In real life, separate was never equal. Perhaps most separate and unequal were the public schools. If you went to a "colored school," you might walk a long way to school.
15 Buses carried white children to schools closer by. Schools for white children would be modern and well maintained. Yours would be old and run-down. White students would have new books. You might share an old textbook with three other students.

20 In 1949, some black parents decided to sue[4] their school district. The district had built a brand-new school for white students. The black students' school was falling apart. The all-white school had a teacher and separate room for each grade. The all-black school had only two teachers and two
25 classrooms for all eight grades.

Finally, in 1954, the Supreme Court ruled in *Brown* v. *Board of Education* that segregated[5] schools were unequal. The old ruling that let people be divided by skin color was gone. Separate could never be equal.

---

1. **Colored:** an offensive word used to describe African Americans.
2. **spigot:** faucet.
3. **civil rights:** personal freedoms.
4. **to sue:** to try to gain a right or to get justice through legal means.
5. **segregated:** set apart from others.

Contrast Chart

When you **contrast** two things, you find the differences between them. The following chart will help you contrast the school experiences of black children to those of white children in "Separate but Never Equal."

First, tell how black children got to school by filling in the "Getting to School" section under "Education for Black Children." Then, tell how white children got to school by filling in the "Getting to School" section under "Education for White Children." Then, fill in the rest of the sections. One contrast has been filled in for you.

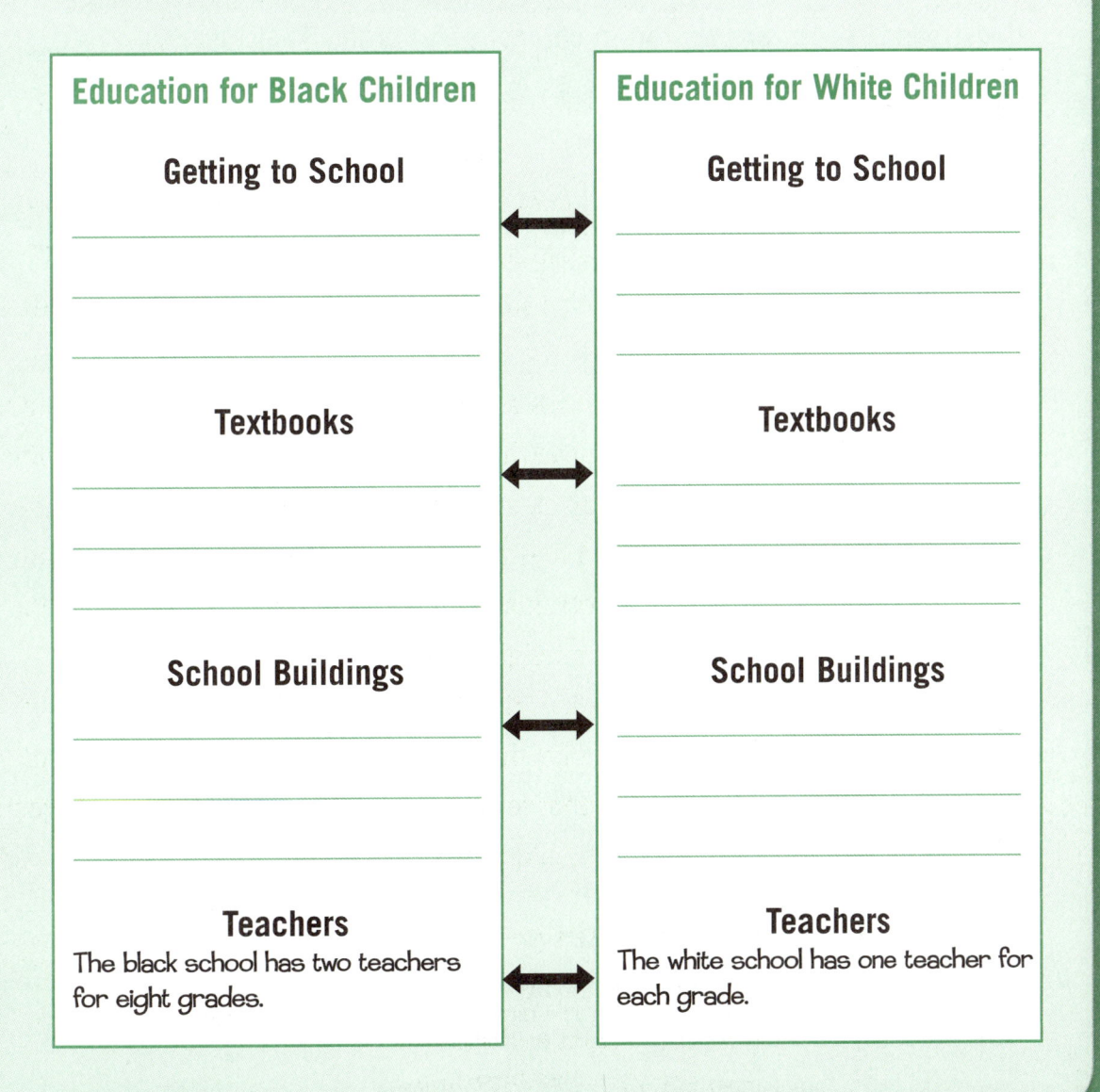

Education for Black Children	Education for White Children
Getting to School	**Getting to School**
Textbooks	**Textbooks**
School Buildings	**School Buildings**
Teachers The black school has two teachers for eight grades.	**Teachers** The white school has one teacher for each grade.

Before You Read

La Bamba

Literary Focus: Short Story

A **short story** is prose fiction that runs from about three to twenty pages. (**Fiction** is something that's made up. **Prose** is any writing that is not poetry.) A short story usually has just one or two main characters and one *conflict,* or problem the character faces.

Reading Skill: Sequencing

Most short stories are written in **chronological** order. That means the writer tells us the events in the order in which they happen. However, sometimes writers use **flashbacks,** events that occur in an earlier time period. As you read "La Bamba," notice the **sequencing**—or order—of events. Look for **time clues** like these:

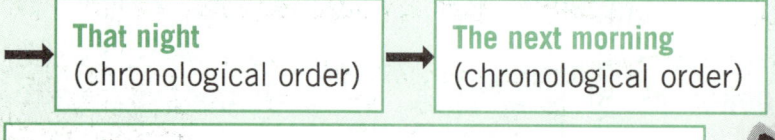

→ | **That night** (chronological order) | → | **The next morning** (chronological order) |

| **In first grade . . .** (Flashback) |

Into the Short Story

"La Bamba" was a hit song in the late 1950s. It was recorded by Ritchie Valens (1941–1959), who was the first Mexican American rock star. In this story, a boy named Manuel decides to perform "La Bamba" for a school talent show. Manuel won't actually sing the song, though. He's going to mouth the words as a record plays. (Records were what people listened to before CDs or MP3s.) Have you ever pretended to sing like that, maybe at a karaoke party? Were you nervous, or did you enjoy all the attention?

La Bamba

Based on the Story by
Gary Soto

Here's HOW

SEQUENCING

The story opens with Manuel walking to school. That must mean the story begins in the morning.

Your TURN

SEQUENCING

In line 10, Manuel shows his act to his friend Benny. Underline the **time clue** in this line. About how many hours have passed since the event in line 1?

_____
_____

Here's HOW

SHORT STORY

OK. I know that short stories usually have only one main character. In this story, that's Manuel.

Your TURN

SHORT STORY

What problem does Manuel face?

_____
_____
_____

---

1   **A**s Manuel walked to school, he thought about tomorrow's talent show. He was amazed that he had volunteered. He was going to pretend to sing Ritchie Valens's "La Bamba" before the whole school.

5   He was nervous. But he longed to be the center of attention. He wanted to impress his friends. He especially wanted to impress Petra Lopez, the second prettiest girl in his class. The prettiest girl was already taken. Since he wasn't great-looking himself, he knew he should be reasonable.

10   At lunch, Manuel showed his act to his friend Benny. Benny was going to play the trumpet in the talent show. Benny watched. He suggested that Manuel should dance.

"Just think like you're Michael Jackson or someone like that," Benny said.

15   Manuel decided that was a good idea.

In the cafeteria, during rehearsal, Mr. Roybal tested the equipment. He cursed under his breath when the record player jammed.[1] He was nervous about directing the talent show.

"Is it broken?" Manuel asked.

20   Mr. Roybal promised Manuel he would have a good record player at the talent show.

Manuel twirled[2] his "La Bamba" record as he watched the other acts rehearse. It looked like it would be a great talent show. His parents would be proud. His brothers and sisters

25 would be jealous. It would be a night to remember.

Benny was about to rehearse his trumpet solo. He blew so loudly that Manuel dropped his record. It rolled across the floor and hit a wall. Manuel grabbed it and wiped it off. He was relieved that it hadn't broken.

---

1. **jammed:** put out of order; broken.
2. **twirled** (twurld): turned around with his fingers; whirled; spun.

"La Bamba" adapted from *Baseball in April and Other Stories* by Gary Soto. Copyright © 1990 by Gary Soto. Retold by Holt, Rinehart and Winston. Reproduced by permission of **Harcourt, Inc.**

30   That night, in bed, Manuel prayed that he wouldn't mess up. He didn't want to embarrass himself, as he did in the first grade, during Science Week. He had made a simple flashlight from a light bulb and a battery. He showed it off to all his neighbors. When it was time to show it to his class, the
35   battery was dead. Some kids snickered[3] at him.

The next morning, Manuel's parents were smiling proudly. They were curious about what he was going to do, but Manuel wanted to surprise them.

The day flew by. Suddenly it was evening, and Manuel
40   was standing backstage in his best clothes. He could hear the crowd filling the cafeteria. Then he heard Mr. Roybal introduce the first act. It was a girl dressed as a toothbrush and a boy dressed as a dirty gray tooth. They sang a little song about brushing and flossing.

45   Next came a mother-daughter violin duo. They got a big round of applause. After that, a group of first-grade girls jumped rope. The crowd was pleased.

Right before Manuel came a karate act. A boy broke a board with his hands. The audience was very impressed.

50   Mr. Roybal announced Manuel's act. Manuel was nervous, but he loved the clapping. The song started up. The shock of standing alone in front of the big crowd made Manuel's first movements stiff. He moved his lips and swayed.[4] Suddenly he noticed his little brother Mario in the audience. Mario was
55   wearing Manuel's favorite shirt. Manuel would deal with him later.

Why am I here? thought Manuel. This is no fun. The audience didn't seem excited at all. But then Manuel did a fancy dance step. The audience clapped. He started to get
60   into a Michael Jackson groove. Suddenly, the record got stuck, and he had to mouth the words

---

3. **snickered** (SNIHK uhrd): laughed in a mean way.
4. **swayed:** moved slowly back and forth.

Your TURN

SEQUENCING

Re-read lines 30–38. Circle the three **time clues**. Which of these **time clues** indicates a **flashback**?

Here's HOW

SEQUENCING

I see another clue that indicates lines 32–33 are a flashback: "He *had* made a simple flashlight." If the event were happening that very night, the verb would be "made," the simple past. The verb "*had* made" shows a past before the past.

Your TURN

SEQUENCING

Circle the **time clues** in lines 39–40. Why do you think the writer doesn't tell us anything about what happened that day? What's the main event of this story?

LA BAMBA   85

Here's HOW

SEQUENCING

The talent show probably lasts only a couple of hours, but it takes up half of the story. That makes sense since the talent show is the climax, or most exciting part, of the story.

Your TURN

SEQUENCING

Look back at the **time clues** in the story. How many days go by from line 1 to the end of the story?

Here's HOW

VOCABULARY

I didn't understand what Manuel was saying in lines 84-85. Then I realized that this explanation isn't supposed to make sense. Manuel is just stringing together fancy technical terms to make himself look smart.

Your TURN

VOCABULARY

In lines 86-87, underline the translation of the Spanish.

Para bailar la bamba
Para bailar la bamba
Para bailar la bamba[5]

65 again and again.

The audience began to laugh and stand on their chairs. Manuel couldn't believe his bad luck. Mr. Roybal brought the record to a sudden stop. All Manuel could do was bow and scoot[6] off stage. The audience clapped wildly, but Manuel felt
70 like crying.

He became angry as he listened to Benny play his trumpet. Benny sounded great. It was Benny's trumpet-playing that had made him drop his record. It must have gotten scratched then. That's why it had skipped.[7]

75 But when the cast lined up for a final bow, Manuel received loud applause that shook the cafeteria walls. Later, everyone patted him on the back. "Way to go. Really funny."

Manuel was confused, but he didn't care. He was the center of attention. Even the popular kids crowded around
80 him. He decided not to punch his brother for wearing his favorite shirt.

That night his father asked him how he had made the needle stick.

"Easy, Dad," said Manuel. "I used laser tracking with high
85 optics and low functional decibels per channel."

"Ay, que niños tan truchas," his father said. "What smart kids. I don't know how you get so smart."

A little later, Manuel, feeling happy, began to sing "La Bamba" into his mirror. But he was tired of the song. He was
90 relieved the day was over. Next year, he thought, he would not volunteer for the talent show. Probably.

---

5. *para bailar la bamba* (PAH rah BY lahr la BAHM bah): Spanish for "to dance the bamba."
6. **scoot:** go suddenly and quickly.
7. **skipped:** The record got stuck and played the same part of the song over and over.

Sequencing: Time Tracker

You just answered many on-page questions about **sequencing** in "La Bamba." Now, review what you learned by completing the chart below. In the boxes that contain **time clues** (1, 3, 5), write what happened in the story. In the boxes that tell what happened in the story (2, 4, 7), write time clues that tell when the event happened. Pay attention: One of the events is a **flashback,** an event that points back to an earlier time. Number 6 has been completed for you.

1. As Manuel walked to school, _____.

2. _____, Manuel showed his act to his friend Benny.

3. That night, _____.

4. _____, Manuel had made a simple flashlight.

5. The next morning, _____.

6. Suddenly it was evening, and Manuel was standing backstage _____.

7. _____ his father asked him how he got the needle to stick.

Medusa's Head

Literary Focus: Mythic Heroes

Who is your favorite superhero? Superman? Wonder Woman? These superheroes have powers to do things humans can't do. In very old stories from Greece, **mythic** (MIHTH ihk) **heroes** are like superheroes. Mythic heroes are powerful people who perform tasks that real humans can't perform. Sometimes Greek gods help mythic heroes in these stories.

Reading Skills: Dialogue with the Text

Having a **dialogue with the text** means noticing the questions that flash through your mind as you read. Questions like these can help you understand what you read:

What does that word mean?

What will happen next?

How do I feel about what just happened?

Into the Greek Myth

The mythic hero in the following story is named Perseus (PUR see uhs). Perseus's task is to cut off the head of Medusa (muh DOO suh). Medusa is a mythical creature called a Gorgon. As you read the story, look for Perseus's heroic deeds. What can he do that other people can't? What help does he get from Greek gods?

Medusa's Head

Based on the Greek Myth Retold by
Olivia Coolidge

Here's How

DIALOGUE WITH THE TEXT

In lines 5–8, I think Zeus pitied Danae because Acrisios was going against the will of the gods.

Your Turn

DIALOGUE WITH THE TEXT

Re-read lines 20–26. Do you think Perseus will return with the Gorgon's head? Why or why not?

_____
_____
_____
_____
_____
_____
_____

---

1 **K**ing Acrisios[1] of Argos[2] was a cruel, selfish man.

The oracle[3] of Apollo[4] had told the king that his daughter, Danae,[5] would have a child who would kill Acrisios. To avoid this fate, the king locked Danae in an underground room.

5 The gods' plans can never be changed. Zeus,[6] king of the gods, pitied Danae. He changed himself into a shower of gold dust. Then he poured himself through a tiny hole in her cell wall.

Acrisios soon learned that Danae had given birth to a son.
10 He didn't dare murder them both. Instead, he put Danae and her baby, Perseus, inside a huge wooden chest. Then he threw the chest into the sea.

The gods made sure the chest landed on an island. A fisherman, Dictys,[7] found the chest. He took Danae and the
15 baby to his brother Polydectes,[8] the king of the island.

Both Dictys and Polydectes fell in love with Danae. Though she preferred Dictys, she was afraid of offending Polydectes. To avoid a conflict, she pretended to care only for her son, Perseus.

20 As Perseus grew up, Polydectes became jealous of Danae's love for her son. So he sent Perseus on a dangerous mission. Perseus was to return with a Gorgon's head.

The Gorgons were three monster sisters with brass hands and gold wings. Two of the Gorgons had scaly heads and
25 fangs. The third one, Medusa, had a beautiful face but snakes instead of hair. Anyone who saw her face turned to stone.

---

1. **Acrisios** (uh CREE see OHS).
2. **Argos** (AR guhs).
3. **oracle** (AWR uh kuhl): a person or place that tells the future.
4. **Apollo** (uh PAHL oh): handsome god of prophecy, medicine, music, and the sun.
5. **Danae** (DAN ay ee).
6. **Zeus** (ZOOS).
7. **Dictys** (DIHK tuhs).
8. **Polydectes** (PAHL ee DEHK teez).

"Medusa's Head" adapted from *Greek Myths* by Olivia Coolidge. Copyright ©1949 and renewed ©1977 by Olivia E. Coolidge. All rights reserved. Retold by Holt, Rinehart and Winston. Reproduced by permission of **Houghton Mifflin Company**.

Perseus prayed to the goddess Athene[9] for help. She offered him a silver shield to use as a mirror. That way he could see Medusa without turning to stone. Athene's brother Hermes[10] gave him a magic sword to kill Medusa.

Athene said, "The sisters called Phorcides[11] *(Fawr suh deez)* will tell you how to reach the nymphs.[12] The nymphs will give you anything else that you need."

Perseus soon found the Phorcides. They were three old women who shared one eye. They continually passed the eye from one to another. Perseus grabbed the eye. He refused to return it. Desperately, they told him where to find the nymphs, so he returned their eye.

The nymphs were happy to help Perseus. They gave him a hat to make him invisible, winged sandals to let him fly, and a sack for Medusa's head. Then Perseus started out to find Medusa.

Finally Perseus came to a great ocean. On the shore, he saw stones shaped like men. They were the men who had looked at Medusa's face. Perseus took out Hermes' sword and dropped onto the shore. The Gorgons lay asleep on the heaped stones.

Two of the Gorgons had nightmare faces. Snakes hissed around the lovely face of the third Gorgon, Medusa. Perseus lifted his sword and stared at her image in his shield. Then he closed his eyes and struck. She screamed and hissed. Perseus grabbed the head by its snaky hair and put it in his sack. Then Perseus flew away, safe from the furious Gorgons.

Perseus flew to the distant west. There he saw the giant Atlas holding the heavens on his shoulders. Weary Atlas begged Perseus to show him Medusa's head. Perseus

---

9. **Athene** (uh THEE nee): goddess of wisdom and the arts.
10. **Hermes** (HUR meez): messenger of the gods, usually wears winged shoes and a cap.
11. **Phorcides** (FAWR suh deez).
12. **nymphs** (nihmfs): minor goddesses of nature.

Here's HOW

MYTHIC HEROES

In lines 39–41, I can tell Perseus is a mythic hero. He is given gifts that make him invisible and allow him to fly.

Your TURN

MYTHIC HEROES

In lines 49–53, circle the sentences that tell you Perseus is a mythic hero.

Your TURN

DIALOGUE WITH THE TEXT

The goddess Athene helps Perseus. Other magical beings help him, too. Do you think he deserves their help? Why or why not?

_____
_____
_____
_____
_____
_____
_____

MEDUSA'S HEAD

Your TURN

DIALOGUE WITH THE TEXT

In lines 70–73, why was Polydectes turned into stone?

_____
_____
_____
_____

Here's HOW

VOCABULARY

What does *prophecy* in line 83 mean? The next sentence says that Perseus killed his own grandfather. Hey! I remember that Acrisios heard an oracle at the beginning of the story. The oracle told what would happen one day. That's probably a *prophecy*— words that tell what will happen in the future. I checked a dictionary, and I was right!

---

uncovered the head, and Atlas was changed to a mountain.

The wind took Perseus south to Ethiopia.[13] Below, he saw a young girl chained to a rock. He landed and learned her story.

60 She was Andromeda,[14] the daughter of Cepheus,[15] the King of Ethiopia. The queen had angered the sea god, Poseidon.[16] Poseidon flooded the land and sent a monster to destroy the coast. To save their country, the king and queen chained Andromeda to the rock as an offering to Poseidon.

65 She was waiting for the monster to kill her.

As the monster neared, Perseus showed it Medusa's head, and the monster turned to stone.

Perseus and Andromeda were married. Then they sailed to Polydectes' kingdom. (Paul ee dehk teez)

70 Perseus was angry with Polydectes for treating Danaë — his mother — badly. He said, "You asked me for the Gorgon's head. Look at it!" Then he took out Medusa's head and turned Polydectes into stone.

Perseus left Dictys to be king of the island. Next, he
75 returned his gifts to the gods and went to visit his grandfather. King Acrisios heard Perseus was coming. The king fled in terror to the land of Larissa.[17]

As it happened, an important athletic contest was taking place in Larissa. Perseus competed at discus throwing[18] there.
80 His discus flew high into the air. A wind carried it to Acrisios. The discus fell on Acrisios's foot. The shock killed the weak, old man.

The prophecy had been carried out. Acrisios had been killed by his own grandson. Perseus and Andromeda became
85 king and queen of Argos. They ruled long and happily.

---

13. **Ethiopia** (EE thee OH pee uh): ancient African country.
14. **Andromeda** (an DRAHM uh duh).
15. **Cepheus** (SEE fee uhs).
16. **Poseidon** (poh SY duhn).
17. **Larissa** (luh RIHS uh).
18. **discus throwing**: sports contest to see who can throw a flat, heavy, flying disk farthest.

Mythic Hero Web

Mythic heroes are powerful people who do things that real people can't do. In "Medusa's Head," Perseus is a mythic hero. What makes him a mythic hero? Fill out the following chart to find out.

First, fill in the circles on the left-hand side of the page. Write down what made Perseus a special baby, a special youth, and a special king. Then, fill in the circles on the right-hand side of the page. Write down three of Perseus's heroic deeds. One circle has been filled in for you.

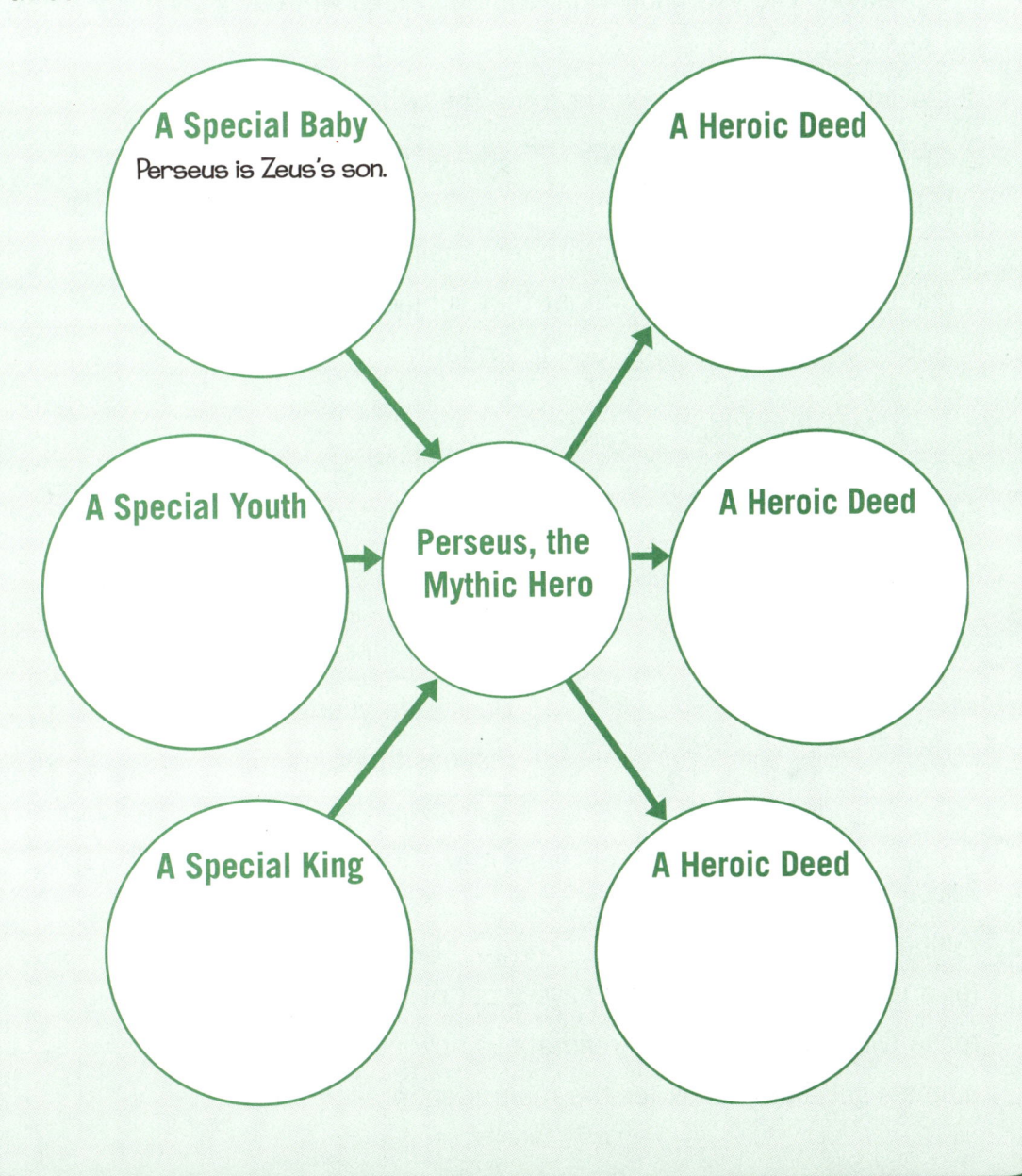

A Special Baby
Perseus is Zeus's son.

A Special Youth

A Special King

Perseus, the Mythic Hero

A Heroic Deed

A Heroic Deed

A Heroic Deed

Medusa's Head

Before You Read

Bringing Tang Home *and* Where the Heart Is

Reading Skill: Main Idea

A **main idea** is the central, most important idea in a piece of writing. Sometimes the main idea is easy to find. Sometimes you have to read more carefully to find it. Here are two helpful questions for finding the main idea:

1. What is the subject of this piece of writing? Answer this question, and you know what the main idea will be about.
2. What is the most important thing the writer has to say about this subject? Answer this question, and you have found the main idea.

Two writers can have two different main ideas about the same subject. If you wrote about that subject yourself, you would have your own main idea to explain.

The subject is

DOGS

Hank writes:

> Dogs are good helpers on the farm and ranch.

Susanna writes:

> Dogs help young children learn responsibility.

Into the Article

People and animals have been living and working together for a long time. Perhaps you have a pet of your own. In these two articles, you will read about how people and animals get along. Look for the main idea in each article.

Bringing Tang Home

Based on the Article by
Gina Spadafori

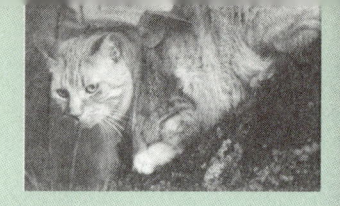

Here's HOW
MAIN IDEA

First, I have to find out what the subject is. The title of this article didn't help much. Who or what is Tang?

Here's HOW
MAIN IDEA

Now, I've read the first few lines. The writer seems to be talking about cats. She's talking about trapping wild cats. Why would anyone want to do that? I'll keep reading.

Your TURN
MAIN IDEA

You know that the article is about trapping and taming wild cats. Read lines 24–27 again. What does the writer want to say about trapping and taming wild cats?

_____
_____
_____
_____
_____

---

1 It is early evening in the woods near my home. There are wild animals there. The woman beside me and I are waiting for animals that should not be wild: We are waiting for cats.

Among the Wild Things

5 Wild animals run away from people. But the feral,[1] or wild, cats are not so eager to run. Perhaps this is because cats and people have been together for a long time. The cats may remember how pleasant it is to be with humans.

The woman with me works to return feral cats to a
10 life with humans. She traps the older ones, has them vaccinated,[2] and has them fixed so they cannot have kittens. Then, she lets them go back to the woods. They are too wild to be good pets. She traps the kittens, tames them, and finds homes for them.

15 Tonight we are after a pale orange tabby[3] named Tang.

The Task of Taming

We can barely see the kitten walk into the trap. He throws himself against the sides of his cage, yowls in fear, and hisses in anger.

20 "Yes!" cries my companion. "We got him!"

Tang is on his way to a home. He will be placed with someone who will love him. He will have a better life than that of a feral cat. Their lives are short and filled with danger.

Feral cats live everywhere. In many places, people try to
25 help the wild cats. Some would rather see the feral cats killed, but these people work to save them.

One kitten at a time, they are making a difference.

---

1. **feral** (FIHR uhl): wild, untamed.
2. **vaccinated** (VAK suh NAYT ed): protected from sickness with a shot.
3. **tabby** (TAB ee): a cat with striped fur.

"Animal Instincts" (retitled "Bringing Tang Home") by Gina Spadafori adapted from *Pets.com, The Magazine for Pets and Their Humans*, vol. 1, issue 4, June 2000. Copyright © 2000 by **Gina Spadafori**. Retold by Holt, Rinehart and Winston. Reproduced by permission of the author.

Where the Heart Is

Based on the Article by
Sheri Henderson

Your TURN

MAIN IDEA

Read the first two paragraphs again. What is the subject of this article?

_____
_____
_____
_____

Your TURN

MAIN IDEA

Sometimes writers wait until the end of a piece to tell the main idea. Read the last four lines. Then, underline the main idea in these lines.

Here's HOW

MAIN IDEA

My teacher asked us, "What main idea do "Bringing Tang Home" and this article have in common?" Well, both articles are about pets. That's the subject they share. The subject isn't the main idea, though. The main idea is what the writers say *about* pets. Let me think about it: Do the writers say something similar about pets?

---

1   On a cold winter night in 1924, a dog limped up to an empty farmhouse. He had lived there once as a pup, but his family had left long ago. The dog had traveled for seven months, his journey[1] taking him across two states. He had
5   swum across the Missouri River. He had crossed the great Rocky Mountains in the middle of winter. He had caught squirrels and rabbits for food. At times strangers had helped him. But always he had traveled on, always heading west.

   In the morning the dog made his way into town and
10 found the house where his people now lived. They had lost him during a vacation. He had walked three thousand miles to find them—to come home.

   How did that dog find his way home? Nobody knows, but many other animals have done the same thing. A cat
15 walked more than a thousand miles to find his family. His journey was to a place where he had never been. A homing pigeon found its owner in a hospital over a hundred miles from home. Some pets know from far away when family members are ill or hurt or in trouble. Others know when
20 members of their family are unexpectedly coming home.

   Some say animals have an extra sense. Humans have five senses—sight, hearing, smell, taste, and touch. Animals could have another sense that connects them to people they love and trust.

25   Perhaps *how* a pet finds us isn't important. A better question may be *why* they find us, even when faced with a long and difficult journey. There's a saying, "Home is where the heart is." For some pets, home is where one person's heart is.

---

1. **journey** (JUR nee): a long trip.

Main Idea

The **subject** of a piece of writing can usually be stated in a word or two: cats, dogs, pets. The **main idea** answers the question "What about it?"—what about cats or dogs or pets? The main idea is the most important thing the writer has to say *about* a subject.

Main-Idea Web

Sometimes you are asked to connect the main ideas in one article to those in another article. Here is a Main-Idea Web that will help you connect "Bringing Tang Home" with "Where the Heart Is."

In the circle on the left, write the main idea in "Bringing Tang Home." In the circle on the right, write the main idea for "Where the Heart Is." Then, in the circle in the middle, write the main idea that both articles share—the connected idea. One circle has been filled in for you.

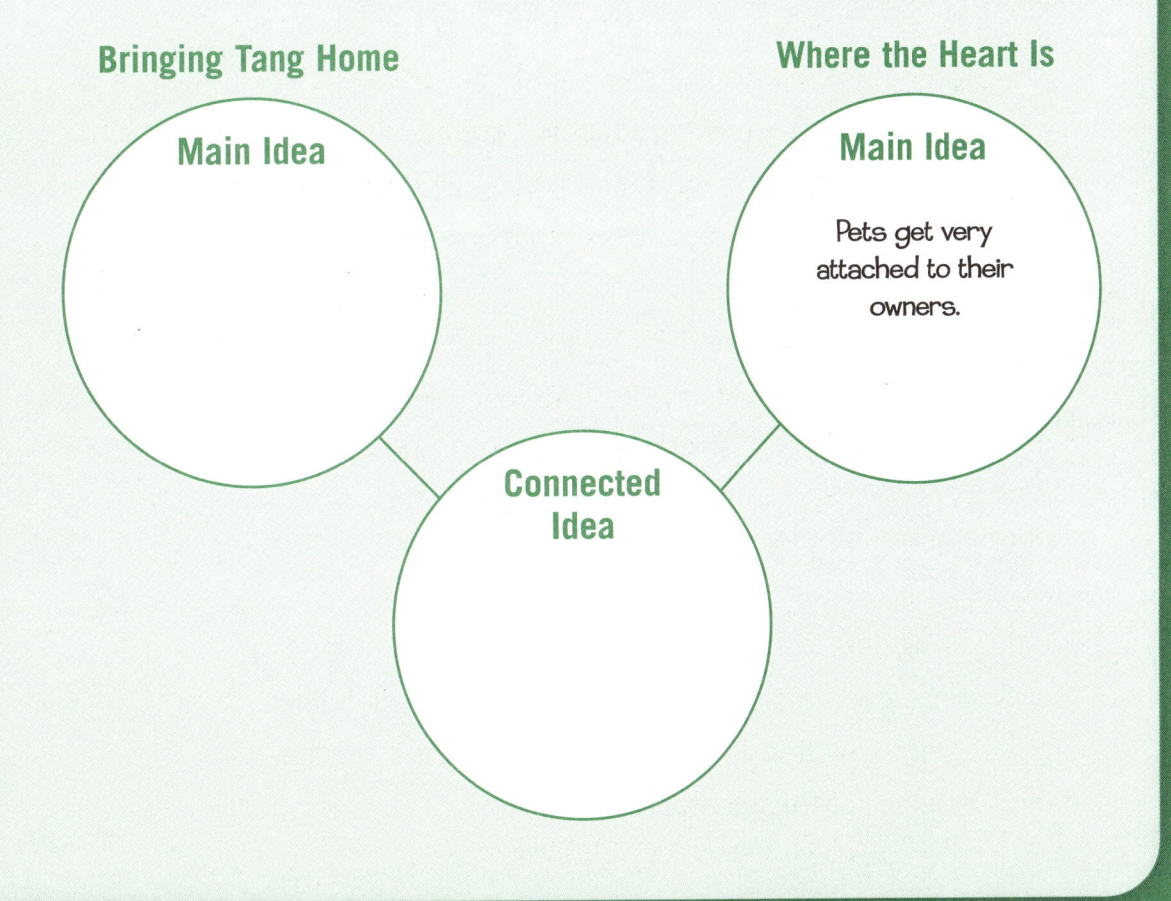

Bringing Tang Home
- Main Idea

Where the Heart Is
- Main Idea: Pets get very attached to their owners.

Connected Idea

Before You Read

Brother

Literary Focus: Description

Description is amazing! It's writing that uses words to help us see, touch, smell, taste, and hear. In "Brother," Maya Angelou paints a word picture of her brother Bailey. He's "small, graceful, and smooth," with "velvet-black skin."

Description is used in all kinds of writing—in fiction, poetry, newspapers, and even e-mail.

Reading Skill: Finding the Main Idea

The **main idea** is the most important idea in a piece of writing. Main ideas are sometimes stated directly. But when a writer doesn't state the main idea, you must figure it out.

Pay close attention to details and key ideas from the text. Then, use those details to guess the larger idea.

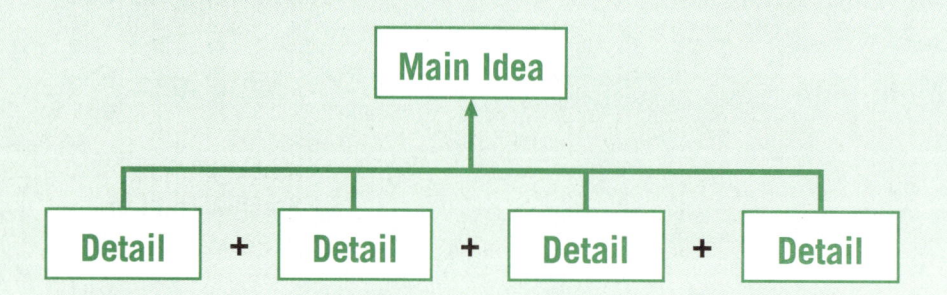

```
                    Main Idea
                        ↑
    ┌───────┬───────┴───────┬───────┐
  Detail + Detail  +  Detail  +  Detail
```

Into the Autobiography

This story is set in the 1930s in Arkansas. At the time, the author and her brother were living with their grandmother "Momma."

Maya Angelou, born in 1928, has had a very interesting life. She has been a singer, a civil rights worker, a college professor, and a writer. In 1993, she read a poem to the nation in honor of President Clinton.

Brother

FROM *I Know Why the Caged Bird Sings*

Based on the Autobiography by **Maya Angelou**

Boy by the Sea (1995) by Jonathan Green, Naples, Florida. Oil on canvas (18" X 17"). Photograph by Tim Stamm.

Here's HOW
FINDING THE MAIN IDEA

I think the main idea is that Bailey was very important to the author. Lots of details in lines 1-8 show how important he was. I underlined some of those details as I was reading.

Here's HOW
VOCABULARY

I'm not sure what *grating* in line 5 means. *Grating* is the last word in Maya's description, and *smooth* is the last word in Bailey's description. The opposite of *smooth* would be "rough." I bet that's the meaning of *grating*.

Here's HOW
VOCABULARY

What does it mean to have a voice "like cooling bacon grease" (line 14) or an "oilier" voice (line 18)? Well, Bailey is being fake polite to the ladies. Having an oily voice must mean he's a smooth talker. He knows how to impress people.

---

1 **B**ailey was the greatest person in my world. He was my brother, my only brother. I had no sisters to share him with. I was so pleased with Bailey that I wanted to be good just to show God that I was grateful. I was big, elbowy,[1] and
5 grating. But he was small, graceful, and smooth. He was praised for his velvet-black skin. His hair fell down in black curls. My head was covered with black steel wool.[2] And yet he loved me.

Our elders sometimes said unkind things about my looks.
10 (My family was so beautiful it hurt me.) But Bailey would wink at me from across the room. Then I knew that soon he would get even. He would let the old ladies finish wondering how on earth I came about. Then he would ask, in a voice like cooling bacon grease, "Oh, Mrs. Coleman, how is your
15 son? I saw him the other day. He looked sick enough to die."

Shocked, the ladies would ask, "Die? From what? He ain't sick."

And in a voice oilier than the one before, he'd answer with a straight face, "From the Uglies."

20 I would hold my laugh. I'd bite my tongue and grit my teeth. Very seriously I'd erase any bit of a smile. Later, we'd laugh and laugh and howl.

Bailey wasn't often punished for such outrageous[3] behavior. He was the pride of our family.

25 He moved like a well-oiled machine. He made time count more than I could. He finished chores, homework, and read more books than I. He played with the best kids in the group games. He could even pray out loud in church. He could steal pickles from under Uncle Willie's nose.

---

1. **elbowy:** clumsy, "all elbows."
2. **steel wool:** rough cleaning pad made of steel shavings.
3. **outrageous:** shocking.

Excerpt (retitled "Brother") adapted from *I Know Why the Caged Bird Sings* by Maya Angelou. Copyright © 1969 and renewed © 1997 by Maya Angelou. Retold by Holt, Rinehart and Winston. Reproduced by permission of **Random House, Inc.**

30   Once when the Store was busy, he fished for two fat pickles. He caught them and left them on the side of the barrel. The pickles dripped until he was ready for them. After school, he picked up the nearly dry pickles. He jammed them into his pockets. We ran out of the Store. It was summer and
35 his pants were short, so the pickle juice made clean streams down his ashy[4] legs. He jumped with his pockets full of loot[5] and his eyes laughing a "How about that?" He smelled like a vinegar barrel or a sour angel.

   After we finished our chores, we were free to play
40 children's games. We had only to stay close enough to hear Uncle Willie's or Momma's call. Playing hide-and-seek, Bailey's voice sang out, "Last night, night before, twenty-four robbers at my door. Who all is hid? Ask me to let them in. Hit 'em in the head with a rolling pin.[6] Who all is hid?" In follow
45 the leader, he made up the boldest and most interesting things to do. And when he was on the tail of the pop the whip,[7] he would twirl off the end like a top. He'd fall spinning and laughing, stopping just before my heart beat its last. Then he was back in the game, still laughing.
50   A lonely child has many needs. The most important need, if there is going to be hope, is a strong God. My pretty black brother was my Kingdom Come.[8]

Here's HOW

DESCRIPTION

Lines 35–36 have a description that uses the sense of sight. I circled the description as I was reading.

Your TURN

DESCRIPTION

Underline a description that uses the sense of smell in lines 37–38.

Your TURN

FINDING THE MAIN IDEA

Now that you've finished reading the selection, what do you think its main idea is? Write your answer below.

_____
_____
_____
_____
_____
_____
_____

---

4. **ashy:** the color of ashes.
5. **loot:** stolen goods.
6. **rolling pin:** tool used to roll out dough by hand.
7. **pop the whip:** children's game. Players form a chain and the leader begins to run. The chain twists and turns as players try to hang on to each other. Finally, the last player in the chain lets go and spins away.
8. **Kingdom Come:** heaven.

Brother from I Know Why the Caged Bird Sings

Description

"Brother" is full of descriptions. These word pictures use our senses of sight, hearing, touch, smell, and taste. Fill in the chart below with details that help us see and hear some of the things described in the story. List one detail each for the senses of sight and hearing. The sense of touch box has been filled in for you.

Detail that we can see:

Detail that we can hear:

Detail that we can touch:
My head was covered with black steel wool.

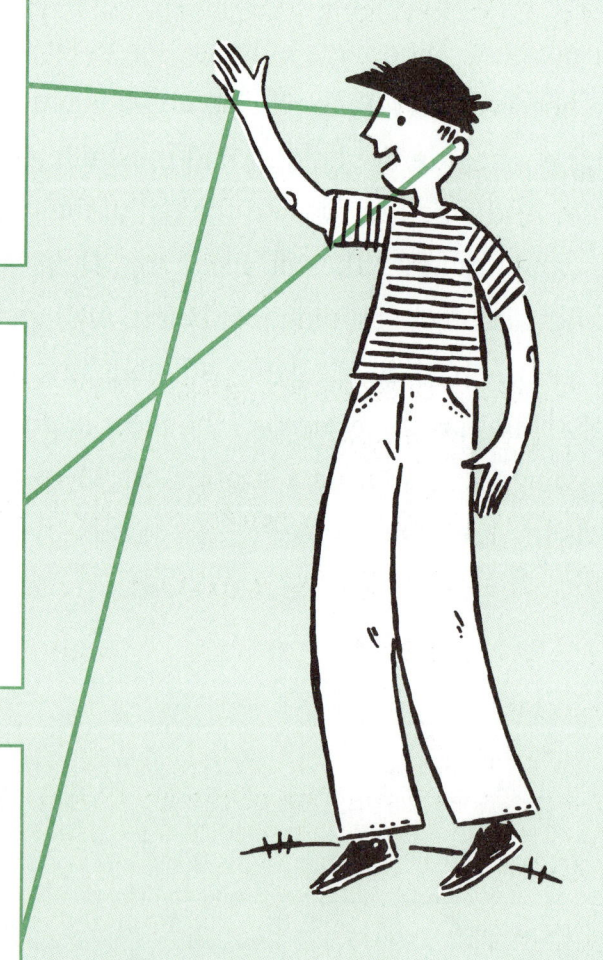

Vocabulary

Synonyms

Synonyms (SIHN uh NIHMZ) are words that have the same or nearly the same meaning. Sometimes, knowing a word's synonym is important. You can use the synonym in your writing. Also, knowing a synonym can help you understand another word's meaning.

A. Match words and synonyms. Write the letter of the correct synonym next to each word. One synonym has been filled in for you.

_____ 1. outrageous   **a.** shocking

__c__ 2. grating   **b.** stolen items

_____ 3. loot   **c.** rough

Word Bank
grating
outrageous
loot

B. Complete each sentence with a word from the Word Bank. One sentence has been completed for you.

1. Maya was big and ___grating___, while Bailey was small and smooth.

2. Bailey ran out of the Store with the _____ in his pockets.

3. Maya loved Bailey's _____ behavior—he could get away with anything!

C. Write a sentence using one of the words from the Word Bank.

My Word: _____

My Sentence: _____

_____

_____

All Aboard with Thomas Garrett

Reading Skill: Main Idea: Stated and Implied

Some informational texts include main-idea statements. Others don't. The two sentences you just read, for example, state this paragraph's main idea. Sometimes, though, the writer leaves it to the reader to get the idea. In these cases, the main idea is **implied,** not stated.

You can figure out implied main ideas by putting together details from the text.

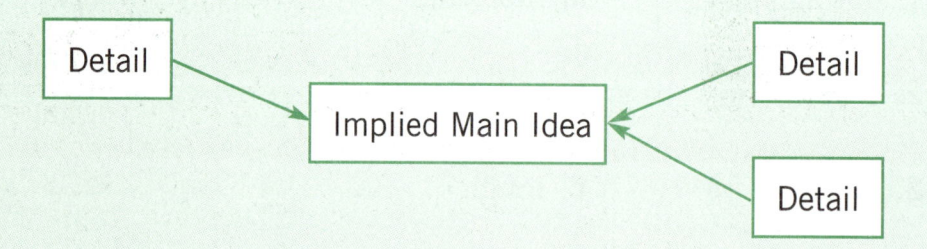

Detail → Implied Main Idea ← Detail
Implied Main Idea ← Detail

Into the Article

You may have never heard of Thomas Garrett. But you probably know about someone else in this article. Harriet Tubman is well known. What can you remember about her?

- She was born a slave.
- She got away to freedom.
- Later, she helped many other slaves get away.

Before you begin reading this article, think about what else you know about slavery in the United States and about the antislavery movement.

All Aboard with Thomas Garrett

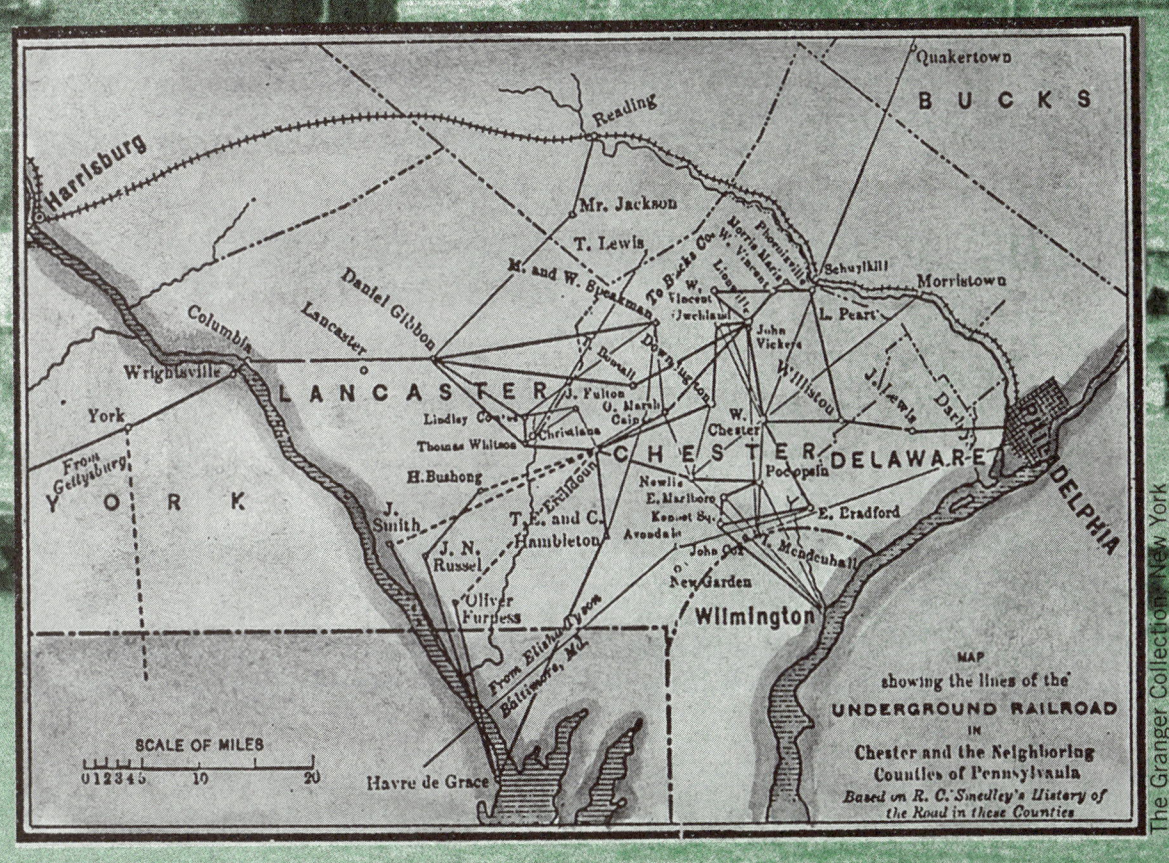

Based on the Article by
Alice P. Miller

1   **T**wo elderly people walked down the front steps of the red brick house. Their clothing showed that they were respectable[1] people. The small lady wore a long gray dress. She carried a snow-white handkerchief. Her bonnet had a
5   veil that hid her face. The tall gentleman wore a long black coat and a hat.

When they reached the sidewalk, the gentleman and lady got into a coach[2] that waited at the curb. At first, the driver drove the horses slowly. Outside Wilmington,[3] the
10 coach moved along at a faster pace. Finally, they crossed into the free state[4] of Pennsylvania.

The tall white man was Thomas Garrett. For many years he had broken the law by helping runaway slaves. The little lady was runaway slave Harriet Tubman, wearing clothes
15 borrowed from Garrett's wife. It was Tubman's first visit to Garrett, but she would return many more times.

Garrett's house was a station on the Underground Railroad. Runaway slaves stayed there a day or two until it was safe to move on. Garrett gave them food, clothing, and
20 new shoes from his shoe store. He made fake passes that gave the runaway slaves written permission to move about freely. The passes helped them get past the police and the slave hunters.

Garrett was not a rich man, but he used his own money
25 to cover[5] his costs. Other people who believed it was wrong to keep slaves also gave him money.

---

1. **respectable** (rih SPEHK tuh buhl): correct in behavior, worthy of trust.
2. **coach** (kohch): an old-fashioned carriage pulled by horses.
3. **Wilmington** (WIL mihng tuhn): a town in Delaware, which was a slave state at that time.
4. **free state:** a state that did not allow slavery.
5. **cover:** to pay for.

"All Aboard with Thomas Garrett" by Alice P. Miller adapted from *Cobblestone*, vol. 2, no. 2, February 1981. Copyright © 1981 by Alice P. Miller. Retold by Holt, Rinehart and Winston. Reproduced by permission of the **Estate of Alice P. Miller.**

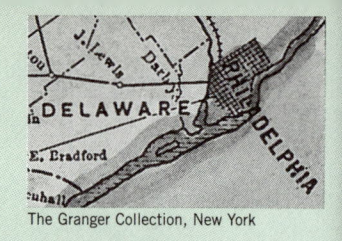

However, there was never enough money. Yet Garrett never turned away a runaway slave. He never refused food to anyone. He would rather have gone hungry himself.

Garrett, who was born in Pennsylvania, had been helping slaves since 1822. That year, he helped a young black woman who was trying to escape from her master. At that time he vowed to spend the rest of his life helping slaves. He remained faithful to that promise.

Garrett ran the best station on the Underground Railroad. It was the station that was used most often. It was also the most dangerous because Wilmington was so close to Pennsylvania, which was a free state. There were many slave catchers in Wilmington. They watched all roads going north to Pennsylvania.

Helping slaves escape was against the law, but Garrett got away with it for a long time. He knew many ways to help slaves hide from the slave catchers. Sometimes he disguised a slave, as he had done with Harriet Tubman. Sometimes he dressed a man in woman's clothing or a woman in man's clothing. Other times he would show a young person how to appear to be old and bent over with age. Another reason for his success was that he had many friends who would hide runaway slaves under a wagonload of vegetables or in a secret compartment[6] in a wagon.

However, in 1848, two slave owners took him to court. A 1793 law punished people who helped runaways. The jury[7] decided in favor of the owners. Garrett had to pay $5,400 in fines.

After the trial ended, Garrett stood up and told the court he would never stop. He said he had already helped

Your TURN

VOCABULARY

Lines 53–54 say Garrett had to pay a fine. What is a fine? Use what you already know to figure it out. You know that Garrett had to go to court. He had broken a law. You also know that Garrett paid $5,400. With this information, you can guess what *fine* means. Write your guess below. Then, check a dictionary. Were you right?

_____

_____

_____

_____

_____

---

6. **compartment** (kuhm PAHRT muhnt): a place for storing things.
7. **jury** (JUR ee): group of people in a law court who decide whether someone is guilty or not guilty.

Your TURN

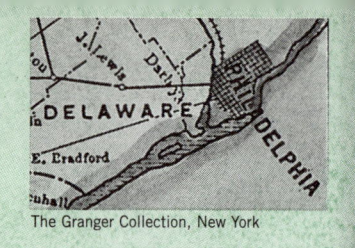

IMPLIED MAIN IDEA

Re-read lines 60–63. What do these details tell you about the strength of Thomas Garrett's beliefs?

_____

_____

_____

fourteen hundred slaves. He promised to double the help he'd given. He had no money left. Even without money, he would go on helping slaves gain freedom.

60 Garrett sold all his furniture, but that was not enough to pay the fine. He borrowed money from his friends and was able to pay the heavy fines. He went on helping slaves reach freedom.

As time went on, Garrett's business grew and he had 65 more money. He paid the money back to his friends. In 1863, slavery in America ended. By then, Garrett had helped more than 2,700 slaves.

Garrett and Harriet Tubman met many times during those years. Tubman made many trips to the South and returned 70 with bands of slaves. Garrett always helped them escape. Garrett wrote many letters to Harriet Tubman. We know much about Tubman from his letters.

Garrett admired Tubman. He wrote that he'd never met anyone like her. He said that Tubman was never afraid 75 because she trusted God and went where He sent her.

In April 1870, the United States passed a law that said that black citizens and citizens who had been slaves could vote. Their right to vote could not be taken away.

Joyful black people pulled Garrett through the streets in 80 an open carriage. On its side, they had written, "Our Moses."[8]

---

8. Moses (MOH zuhz): strong leader of ancient times who helped the Jewish people gain freedom from slavery in Egypt.

Implied Main Idea

An **implied main idea** is a main idea just waiting to be discovered. Complete the organizer below by filling in details and implied main ideas from the text. Some ideas and details are already filled in. (You can use details from the Here's How and Your Turn items, also.) Then, put the main ideas together to come up with the overall main idea. Try stating the overall main idea this way: "Because [or In spite of] _____, Garrett_____."

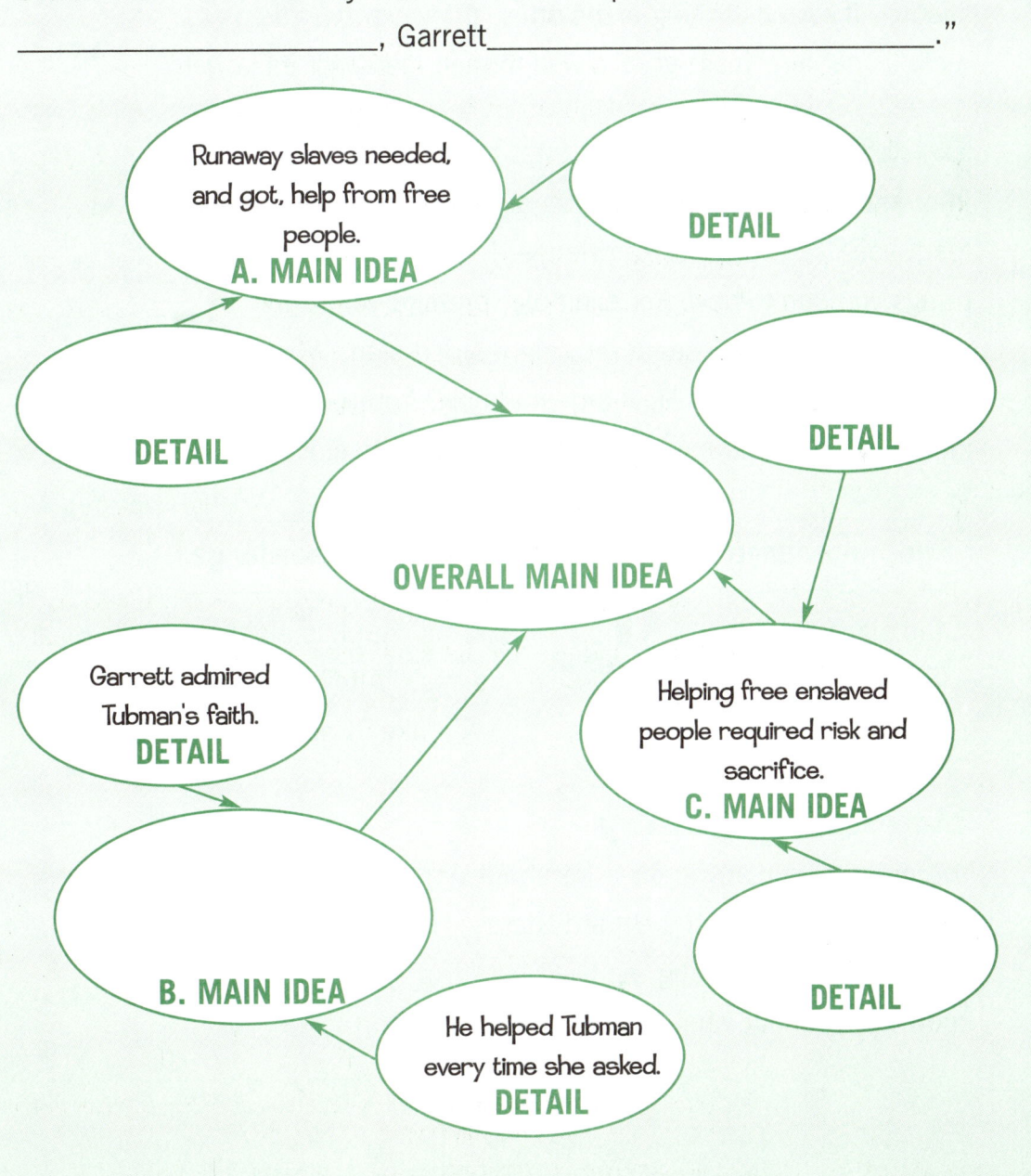

- Runaway slaves needed, and got, help from free people.
  A. MAIN IDEA

- **DETAIL**

- **DETAIL**

- **DETAIL**

- **OVERALL MAIN IDEA**

- Garrett admired Tubman's faith.
  DETAIL

- **B. MAIN IDEA**

- He helped Tubman every time she asked.
  DETAIL

- Helping free enslaved people required risk and sacrifice.
  C. MAIN IDEA

- **DETAIL**

Before You Read

The Mysterious Mr. Lincoln

Literary Focus: Metaphor

"I fly on my skateboard." "My grandmother is a rock." Sentences like these make you compare things that might seem to have little in common. *A skateboard and flying? Grandma and a rock?* These types of comparisons are called **metaphors.** A metaphor does not just say one thing *is like* another. It says that thing *is* the other. (*"My grandmother is a rock."*) That directness gives a well-formed metaphor its power.

Reading Skill: Using Prior Knowledge

Prior knowledge is something you already know. When you read, you use your prior knowledge. It helps you figure out things you don't know. For example, pretend you're in another country. You see a red, eight-sided sign. What does it say? It says "Stop." How did you know? You used prior knowledge about stop signs to tell you what it said.

Prior Knowledge		Using Prior Knowledge	
Stop signs are red. Stop signs have eight sides.	ALTO	This sign has eight sides. "Alto" sounds like "Halt."	→ This sign means "Stop."

Into the Biography

You probably already know a lot about Abraham Lincoln. He was President of the United States. He freed the slaves. He led the Union during the Civil War. But, you might not know much about what he was like as a person.

The Mysterious Mr. Lincoln

President Lincoln's first Home in Illinois.

Based on the Biography by
Russell Freedman

Here's HOW

METAPHOR

Line 6 says Lincoln "towered" over people. *Towering* makes me think of a building at first, not a person. I'm picturing Lincoln being so tall that he casts a shadow over everything around him. That's a good metaphor.

Your TURN

METAPHOR

Re-read lines 20–22. What picture pops into your mind when you think of an artist trying to *capture* Lincoln? Now fill in the blanks below. There's no one "correct" answer. Let your imagination run wild!

In this metaphor, an artist trying to paint a picture of Lincoln makes me think of a _____ trying to capture a _____.

---

1   **A**braham Lincoln wasn't the kind of man who could get lost in a crowd. After all, he stood six feet four inches tall. His high silk hat made him seem even taller.

    Much of his height was in his long, bony legs. When 5 sitting in a chair, he seemed no taller than other people. It was only when he stood up that he towered above[1] others.

    Most people thought that Lincoln was homely.[2] He agreed. He once called his face poor and lean.[3] He learned to laugh at his own gawky looks. One time a man called him 10 "two-faced."[4] Lincoln replied: "I leave it to my audience. If I had another face, do you think I'd wear this one?"

    Those who knew him called Lincoln a man of many faces. He sometimes looked sad and gloomy. The photo process of his day may have added to this look. Taking 15 photos took a long time. The person being photographed had to "freeze" for several seconds. So in photos, Lincoln looks stiff and serious. We never see him laughing. In person, though, he was lively and witty. When he smiled, his face changed. Suddenly he could look quite handsome.

20   When artists and writers tried to show the "real" Lincoln, they always missed something. No one seemed able to capture him.

    Today it's hard to imagine Lincoln as he really was. Even his closest friends never fully understood him. To 25 many people, Lincoln was a mystery. He was a talker, but he kept his feelings to himself. Lincoln's life story has been

---

1. **towered above:** was much taller than.
2. **homely:** plain, unattractive.
3. **lean:** skinny, too thin.
4. **two-faced:** dishonest.

"The Mysterious Mr. Lincoln" adapted from *Lincoln: A Photobiography* by Russell Freedman. Copyright © 1987 by Russell Freedman. All rights reserved. Retold by Holt, Rinehart and Winston. Reproduced by permission of **Clarion Books/Houghton Mifflin Company.**

told many times. He has become an American legend. But the legend partly hides the flesh-and-blood[5] man.

The legendary Lincoln was called Honest Abe, a man of the people. We know that Lincoln was a poor boy who made good.[6] He went from a log cabin to the White House. His manners always were folksy. He called his wife "mother." He wore slippers when he greeted important people. He invited guests to "stay a spell."[7] He told jokes at cabinet meetings.[8]

Lincoln seemed to be a common man, but he was not. He worked hard all his life to get ahead. By the time he ran for president, he had become wealthy. He earned a large income from his law practice and from investments. Lincoln was proud of his success.

He hated the nickname Abe. People who knew him well did not call him that to his face. His friends called him Lincoln or Mr. Lincoln.

Some writers described Lincoln as a sloppy dresser. That was not true, either. In fact, he bought two suits a year from the best tailor[9] in Springfield, Illinois. In those days, many men lived, died, and were buried in the same suit.

Lincoln attended school for only a short time. He taught himself almost everything he learned. The way he said certain words sounded funny to some people. He'd say "git" for *get* and "thar" for *there*. However, he became one of the world's great speakers. Everyone listened when he spoke. Today people still remember his carefully chosen words.

Your TURN

VOCABULARY

In line 32, the writer says Lincoln was *folksy*. Lines 32–35 describe how "folksy" people act. Finish this sentence: "A folksy person is

_____
_____
_____
_____
_____."

Here's HOW

USING PRIOR KNOWLEDGE

I know that sometimes people look down on another person who has a different accent. Maybe they think the accent means the other person isn't well-educated. I wonder if Lincoln used his accent to win arguments. Maybe other people would start out thinking he was a fool, then realize that they'd been fooled by his accent.

---

5. **flesh-and-blood:** living, real.
6. **made good:** rose above poverty, became successful.
7. **stay a spell:** stay for a while.
8. **cabinet meetings:** meetings with official advisors to the President.
9. **tailor:** someone who makes and repairs clothes.

Your TURN

VOCABULARY

Union can mean "a group of workers" or "a group of states." Which meaning do you think is correct in line 67?

___

Your TURN

USING PRIOR KNOWLEDGE

Lines 71–72 say that Frederick Douglass was a slave who escaped. Think about what you know about slavery. Then, even if you don't know anything about Douglass, think about why a former slave might have doubted Lincoln. Write your thoughts on the lines below.

___

Lincoln was famous for his funny stories. But often he
55 was sad and moody. A friend said Lincoln told tall tales to "whistle down sadness."[10]

He showed a lawyer's cool logic. He faced problems with common sense. Yet he believed that dreams could tell the future.

60 Today, we admire Lincoln as an American folk hero. But during the Civil War many disliked him. His enemies called him a hick[11] and a stupid baboon who did not deserve to be president. Others praised him, saying he had saved the United States.

65 Lincoln is known for freeing the slaves. But he did not start with that goal in mind. At first, he wanted only to save the Union. As the war went on, his ideas changed. He felt that owning people was wrong. He believed that the Union had to win to wipe out the sin of slavery.

70 Early in the war, Frederick Douglass, a black leader and writer, was critical of Lincoln. Douglass, a former slave who had escaped to the North, called Lincoln the "white man's president." He thought Lincoln did not care about the slaves. Later, Douglass changed his mind.

75 After the war, Douglass said that Lincoln had done two things. First, he had saved the Union. Second, he had freed the United States from slavery. Douglass said there was no one in the world "better fitted for his mission than Abraham Lincoln."

---

10. **whistle down sadness:** make himself happy.
11. **hick:** hillbilly, country bumpkin.

Prior-Knowledge Web

The author of this biography says that Abraham Lincoln was "mysterious" and hard to understand. But the author tells readers a lot about Lincoln. Use the web below to understand Lincoln better. First, fill in the box that asks about your **prior knowledge**—what you already knew about Lincoln. Then, fill in the remaining boxes. Finally, fill in the middle circle with your own ideas about what Lincoln was like. One box has been filled in for you.

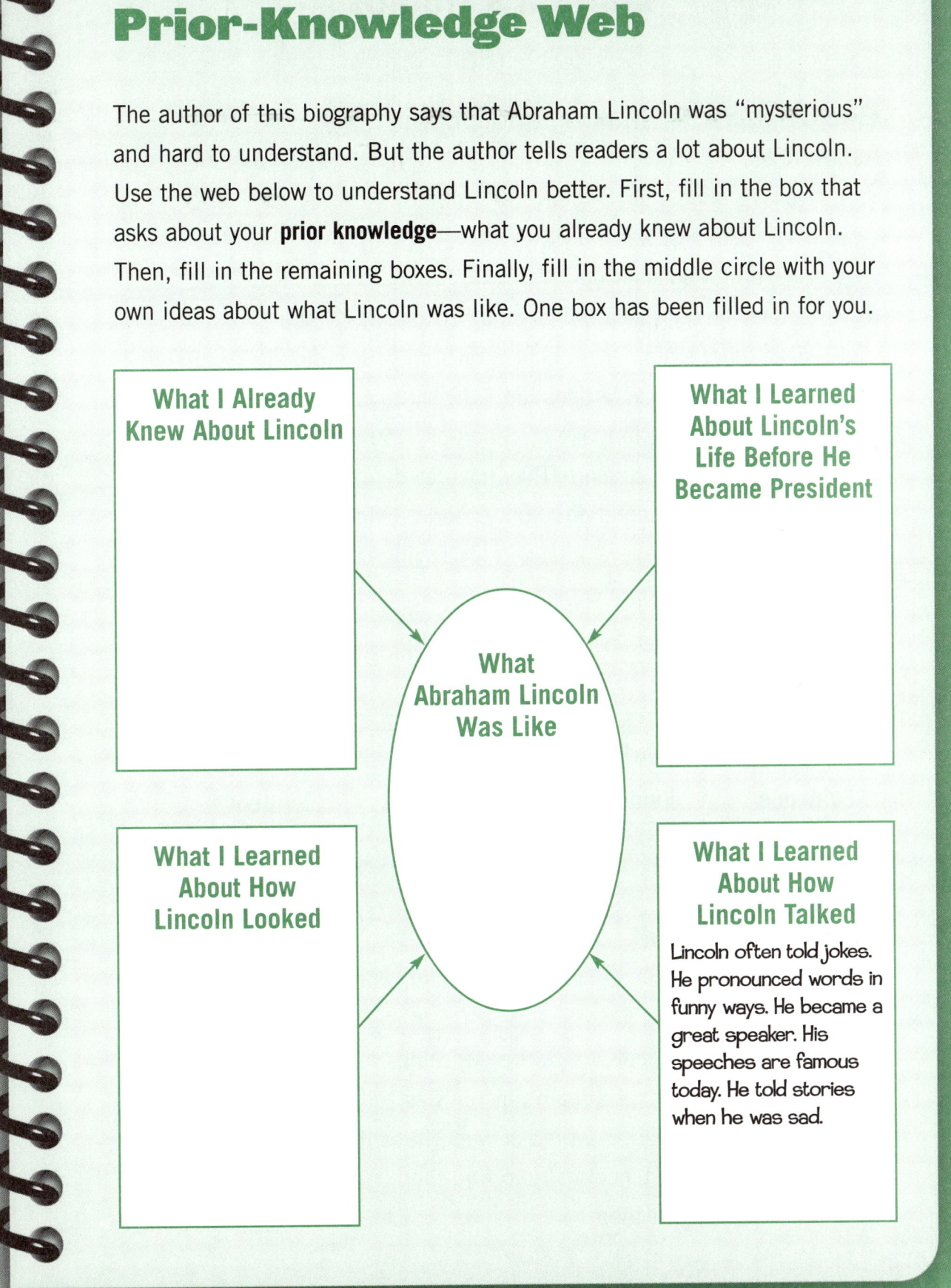

What I Already Knew About Lincoln

What I Learned About Lincoln's Life Before He Became President

What Abraham Lincoln Was Like

What I Learned About How Lincoln Looked

What I Learned About How Lincoln Talked

Lincoln often told jokes. He pronounced words in funny ways. He became a great speaker. His speeches are famous today. He told stories when he was sad.

THE MYSTERIOUS MR. LINCOLN

Before You Read

Lincoln's Humor

Reading Skill: Making and Supporting Assertions

- "Jackie's such a good friend."
- "That math test was easy!"
- "I need new shoes soon."

You might say any of these things on a school day. Or you might make other statements about what's on your mind. These are examples of **assertions** (uh SUR shuhnz).

It's not enough just to make an assertion. You can't quit there. Assertions need support. They need evidence, such as examples, facts, and quotations from experts. Evidence helps your audience believe what you are saying. Evidence makes your assertion more convincing.

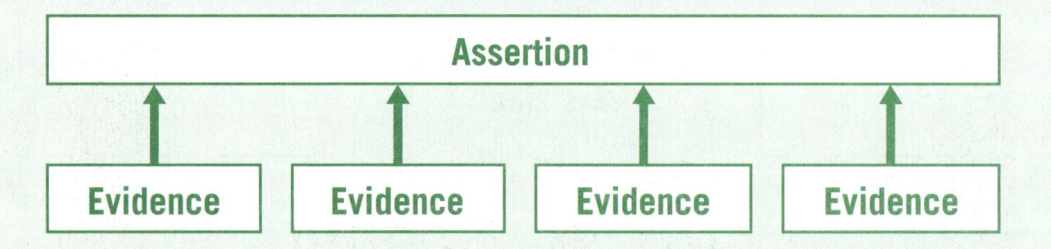

```
                  Assertion
         ↑        ↑        ↑        ↑
      Evidence Evidence Evidence Evidence
```

Into the Article

What kind of humor do you like? Do you laugh when someone on TV slips on a banana peel? Or do you say, "That's just dumb." People find different things funny. Now read "Lincoln's Humor." Abraham Lincoln was the President of the United States during a time of war. The writer makes some assertions about Lincoln. Try to find them. Then, look for evidence to support them.

Lincoln's Humor

Based on the Article by
Louis W. Koenig

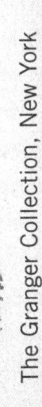

VOCABULARY

Here's a new word in line 1. What does *humorist* mean? I see the word *humor* in it. That means funny stuff. Let me think. What does *–ist* mean? I know some words that end that way. A cyclist rides a bicycle. A guitarist plays guitar. Maybe a humorist is someone who tells jokes.

SUPPORTING ASSERTIONS

In the first paragraph, the writer makes an assertion that Lincoln could tell a joke. I've underlined that assertion. Now, I'll circle the evidence in the first paragraph that the writer gives to support that assertion. I'm going to look for more evidence as I read.

---

1   Lincoln was the White House's first and best humorist. Lincoln had many worries because he was president during a war, but Lincoln could laugh, joke, and tell stories. One friend said he could make a cat laugh. Lincoln thought
5   laughing made life easier and more joyous.

Lincoln was a lawyer and a politician.[1] In both jobs, he told funny stories for many reasons: to make important points, to make people feel comfortable, or to change the subject. He even used body language[2] to make people
10 laugh.

Lincoln used humor to show when his political opponents[3] were wrong. These opponents did not like Lincoln's humor. Stephen A. Douglas was Lincoln's opponent in a race for the Senate. He said that all Lincoln's stories
15 seemed like a blow to his back.

Here are some funny things Lincoln said.

• When Lincoln was a lawyer, he defended a farmer in court. The farmer had been attacked by his neighbor's dog, so the farmer had poked the dog with a pitchfork.[4] The dog's
20 owner was very angry. The dog owner's lawyer said the farmer should have used the handle end of the pitchfork to avoid hurting the dog. If so, Lincoln said, then the dog should have approached the farmer with *its* back end.

• When Lincoln was president, many people came to ask
25 for favors. One time, Lincoln showed one of these visitors a rash on his hand. Though it was only a mild case of smallpox, the visitor left quickly.

---

1. **politician** (PAH luh TIHSH uhn): a person taking part in governing a nation, state, or city.
2. **body language:** a way of getting information across by using hands, face, and posture; for example, crossing your arms and frowning to show anger.
3. **opponents** (uh POH nuhnts): people who act against another person.
4. **pitchfork:** large fork with a long handle used to toss hay.

Lincoln said to his doctor, "There's one good thing about this. I now have something I can give to everybody."

30 • During the Civil War, Lincoln asked his generals for many progress reports. One general was very bothered by this. He sent a telegram to the White House. It said, "We have just caught six cows. What shall we do with them?"

Lincoln answered, "Milk them."

Your TURN

SUPPORTING ASSERTIONS

The writer tells three stories that are supposed to show that Lincoln was funny. Circle these three stories and label them 1, 2, and 3.

Your TURN

SUPPORTING ASSERTIONS

Do you think the writer gives good evidence to support his assertion? Choose one of the three examples of Lincoln's humor. Read it again. Explain why you think it is, or isn't, funny.

_____
_____
_____
_____
_____
_____
_____
_____
_____
_____
_____
_____
_____

LINCOLN'S HUMOR

Lincoln's Humor

Supporting Assertions

"Humor makes the world a better place." This is an **assertion,** a statement that may or may not be true. Maybe you agree with this assertion, or maybe you don't. If someone wants to persuade you that the assertion is true, he or she will need to present some evidence. Evidence could be a quotation from an expert: "Dr. Kelley says that laughter is good for your health." Evidence could be a fact: "Humor helps people feel better about themselves." Evidence could be an example: "I always feel better and kinder when I hear a joke." Supporting details, or **evidence,** make the assertion more believable.

Mix-and-Match Activity

The writer of "Lincoln's Humor" makes an assertion. He says that Lincoln was very funny. Then, the writer gives evidence to support this assertion.

On the left are supporting details, or evidence, about Lincoln's humor. On the right are three assertions. Draw an arrow from each detail to the assertion it supports. One has been done for you.

DETAIL

Lincoln used humor in court.

Lincoln teased a farmer about his dog.

Lincoln used humor with his generals.

Lincoln used humor to make life easier.

Lincoln used humor to get elected.

Lincoln used humor in the White House.

ASSERTION

Lincoln used humor with many different people.

Lincoln used humor in many different places.

Lincoln used humor for many different reasons.

Vocabulary

Context Clues

Word Bank
humorist
opponent
pitchfork

Context clues are words in a sentence that surround a word you don't know. If you know these surrounding words, they can help you understand the meaning of the word that you don't know.

Use context clues in the sentences below to help you complete the sentences. First, read the sentences and notice the two choices in parentheses. Then, look for and underline any context clues. Finally, circle the correct word or words. One has been done for you.

1. The (dogcatcher, humorist) Mark Twain made so many people laugh.

2. Jamal <u>beat</u> his ((opponent), teammate) in the <u>tennis match</u>.

3. The farmer used his (pencil, pitchfork) to toss the hay.

Choose a word from the Word Bank. Use this word to write your own sentence.

My Word: _____

My Sentence: _____

_____

LINCOLN'S HUMOR

Getting Leftovers Back on the Table

Reading Skill: Making Assertions

"Mr. Johnston is a good science teacher," Sarah tells her friend.

Sarah has said something that may or may not be true. In other words, Sarah has made an **assertion**.

Sarah explains her assertion: "Mr. Johnson doesn't give a lot of homework. And he makes science really interesting! Like the other day, he showed us how to make a battery."

Now Sarah has done more than make an assertion. She has explained it. She has supported it with facts.

Mr. Johnson is a good science teacher.

Why do you think so?

Into the Article

The next time you go the lunchroom, look in the trash cans. What do you see? You probably see a lot of food. "What a waste!" you may think. You are about to read an article about a sixth-grader who didn't like to see wasted food, either. He decided to keep food out of the trash can.

Getting Leftovers Back on the Table

Based on the Article by
Mara Rockliff

1   What happens to leftover food? Every day, school cafeterias throw away food. Restaurants and grocery stores do, too. About 20 percent of U.S. food is wasted. Yet, millions of Americans go to sleep hungry.

5   Too big a problem for one kid? A sixth-grader named David Levitt didn't think so. He started small in his own Florida school. Three years later, David was at the White House.[1]

Getting Started

10 David noticed leftover school food was thrown away. He thought homeless shelters[2] could use the leftovers. The school principal explained that health department[3] rules were strict.[4] The leftovers had to be thrown away.

Beating the Odds

15 David didn't give up. He read about a group in Kentucky. This group gave restaurant leftovers to charities.[5] He then presented his own plan to the school board. The board approved his plan—for every school in the county! "It just took a kid to make them see this matters," David
20 says.

Victory at Last

David's program had to meet health department rules. So, he asked companies for special food bags. Soon his program had given hungry people 250,000 pounds of food.
25 Later, David worked on another plan. He wanted to start programs all over Florida. One spring, David went to Washington, D.C., for an award. While at the White House, David met the First Lady.[6] He asked, "What do you do with the White House leftovers?"

---

1. **White House:** the home of the President of the United States and his family.
2. **homeless shelters:** places where people without homes can stay.
3. **health department:** part of the government that deals with health issues.
4. **strict** (strihkt): exact, firm—as in rules that must never be broken.
5. **charities** (CHAR ih teez): groups of people that help people in need of food, clothing, and shelter.
6. **First Lady:** the title given to the wife of the President of the United States.

Assertions Web

An **assertion** is something you say that may or may not be true. You need to support an assertion to persuade people that your assertion *is* true. Good writers support their assertions with interesting facts.

Below is an assertion about the article you just read. Write reasons that support that assertion in the circles below. One has been done for you.

Assertion: David's success shows that teens can make a difference.

Because:
_____
_____
_____

Because:
_____
_____
_____

Because: Adults tried to do the same thing as David. But it took a kid to make the school see that throwing out leftovers was a problem.

Before You Read

John Henry

Literary Focus: Refrain

A **refrain** is a repeated group of words or lines in a poem or song. Think of one of your favorite songs. Does it have a repeated section? If so, that section is a **refrain**. Refrains are often the catchy parts of a song or poem that keep you humming.

Reading Skill: Questioning the Text

Have you ever asked a poem a question? Wondered what part of it means? Told it to explain itself? Believe it or not, **questioning a text** is one of the best ways to understand and enjoy it.

What just happened? What does that mean? Why did it say that? Huh?

Asking questions is easy. Just read along until you have a question. Then, stop and look for the answer to your question. Finally, go back to reading—until you have another question!

Into the Poem

Nobody knows for sure whether John Henry was a real person. People began singing this song about him in the 1870s—over one hundred years ago! In the song, John Henry is an African American worker who uses his hammer to dig a tunnel. Someone sets up a contest between John Henry and a steam drill, a machine that cuts through rock. Who will win? Read the poem, and find out.

John Henry

**Anonymous
African American**

Here's HOW

QUESTIONING THE TEXT

I have a question about lines 1–5. John Henry is a baby, but he picks up a hammer and a piece of steel. Then he starts talking. I don't get it. How could a baby do that? I'll bet the lines show that John Henry was born to dig tunnels—not that he really could talk or pick up a hammer. I'll bet they mean he's going to spend his whole life digging tunnels.

Here's HOW

REFRAIN

I can see the refrain in this song. In each section, the fifth line repeats some of what the fourth line says. I circled the refrains in two of the sections.

Your TURN

REFRAIN

Circle the refrain in lines 16–20.

---

1 John Henry was about three days old
Sittin' on his papa's knee.
He picked up a hammer and a little piece of steel
Said, "Hammer's gonna be the death of me, Lord, Lord!
5 Hammer's gonna be the death of me."

The captain said to John Henry,
"Gonna bring that steam drill 'round
Gonna bring that steam drill out on the job
Gonna whop that steel on down, Lord, Lord!
10 Whop that steel on down."

John Henry told his captain,
"A man ain't nothin' but a man
But before I let your steam drill beat me down
I'd die with a hammer in my hand, Lord, Lord!
15 I'd die with a hammer in my hand."

John Henry said to his shaker,[1]
"Shaker, why don't you sing?
I'm throwing thirty pounds from my hips on down[2]
Just listen to that cold steel ring, Lord, Lord!
20 Listen to that cold steel ring."

John Henry said to his shaker,
"Shaker, you'd better pray
'Cause if I miss that little piece of steel
Tomorrow be your buryin' day, Lord, Lord!
25 Tomorrow be your buryin' day."

---

1. **shaker:** worker who holds the drill for John Henry to strike.
2. **throwing thirty pounds from my hips on down:** a description of John Henry's movement as he swings the thirty-pound hammer.

The shaker said to John Henry,
"I think this mountain's cavin' in!"
John Henry said to his shaker, "Man,
That ain't nothin' but my hammer suckin' wind, Lord,
   Lord!
30 Nothin' but my hammer suckin' wind."

The man that invented the steam drill
Thought he was mighty fine
But John Henry made fifteen feet
The steam drill only made nine, Lord, Lord!
35 The steam drill only made nine.

John Henry hammered in the mountain
His hammer was striking fire
But he worked so hard, he broke his poor heart
He laid down his hammer and he died, Lord, Lord!
40 He laid down his hammer and he died.

John Henry had a little woman
Her name was Polly Ann
John Henry took sick and went to his bed
Polly Ann drove steel like a man, Lord, Lord!
45 Polly Ann drove steel like a man.

John Henry had a little baby
You could hold him in the palm of your hand
The last words I heard that poor boy say,
"My daddy was a steel-driving man, Lord, Lord!
50 My daddy was a steel-driving man."

Your TURN

QUESTIONING THE TEXT

In lines 26–30, what causes the shaker to think the mountain is caving in?

_____
_____
_____
_____

QUESTIONING THE TEXT

Who won the competition between John Henry and the steam drill? Underline the words in lines 31–35 that tell you who won.

REFRAIN

This song is fun to read aloud. Pick four stanzas you like, and read them aloud. Try to read them so that the refrain sounds different from the rest of the stanza.

JOHN HENRY 131

Here's HOW

REFRAIN

I couldn't tell why every fourth line of the poem ends with "Lord, Lord!" Then, I read it aloud. In the lines, "Lord, Lord" reminds me of the sound of two blows of a hammer on steel. I'll bet that's why "Lord, Lord!" is part of the refrain—it's part of John Henry's "steel-driving"!

They took John Henry to the graveyard
And they buried him in the sand
And every locomotive comes a-roaring by
Says, "There lies a steel-driving man, Lord, Lord!
55 There lies a steel-driving man."

Well, every Monday morning
When the bluebirds begin to sing
You can hear John Henry a mile or more
You can hear John Henry's hammer ring, Lord, Lord!
60 You can hear John Henry's hammer ring.

Questioning the Text

When you **question the text,** you stop and ask questions as you read. Then, you think about answers to your questions.

The following chart can help you understand "John Henry." First, read the questions in the box on the left. Then, re-read the lines of the poem. Finally, fill in your answers. One answer has been filled in for you.

Why does John Henry say, "Tomorrow be your buryin' day" if he misses the drill? (lines 21–25) →	
What do you think "broke" John Henry's "poor heart"? (line 38) →	
What might have caused Polly Ann to start digging tunnels when John Henry got sick? (lines 41–45) →	
The speaker hears John Henry's son say, "My daddy was a steel-driving man." Was John Henry's son a baby when he said this? (lines 46–50) →	I don't know! Maybe he was grown up when he said it. Maybe not. I'll bet it doesn't matter. I'll bet the line shows how proud he was of his father.

Before You Read

The Dog of Pompeii

Literary Focus: Credible Characters

Have you ever cared deeply about the characters in a story? Maybe you even felt as if these characters were part of your own life. If so, you've found *credible,* or believable, characters. **Credible characters** are true to life. It's as if you really know them.

Reading Skills: Making Inferences

When you read a story, you make **inferences**, or educated guesses. You guess what will happen next. You guess about things the writer has left out. You base your guesses on what you already know and on details in the story.

What I Know	Story Details	Inference
Some dogs can sense natural disasters before they happen.	The dog in this story begins to act strangely.	Maybe this dog is sensing the volcano is about to erupt.

Into the Short Story

This story is about a blind boy named Tito and his dog Bimbo. The story takes place long ago in Pompeii (pahm PAY), a city in Italy. Pompeii was destroyed more than 1,900 years ago by a volcano. In two days, volcanic ash and other material buried the city. But this material also saved the city. Scientists were able to find houses, artwork, and streets under the volcanic material. These things can still be seen today.

THE DOG OF POMPEII

Based on the Story by
Louis Untermeyer

Here's HOW

CREDIBLE CHARACTERS

This story takes place a long time ago, in Roman times. I wonder if I can care about the characters since their lives are so different from mine. Well, I already like Tito because he loves his dog. I love my dog, too!

Your TURN

MAKING INFERENCES

Re-read lines 10–15. Why do you think Tito and Bimbo are so close to one another?

---

1 **T**ito and his dog Bimbo lived in the old town of Pompeii. Pompeii was a happy place. The streets were lively with shining chariots.[1] The open-air theaters and all sports events were free. Every year, Caesar, the Roman emperor,[2] visited
5 the city. Fireworks honored him for days.

Tito saw none of Pompeii's wonders[3] because he had been blind from birth. No one remembered his parents. People remembered seeing Tito and Bimbo together for about thirteen years.

10 Bimbo was not only Tito's dog. He was Tito's mother, father, nurse, pillow, and playmate. Bimbo left Tito only three times a day. Every morning, while Tito still slept, Bimbo disappeared. When Tito woke, Bimbo would be back, sitting quietly. At his feet, he'd have a large roll of fresh-baked
15 bread. Then, Tito and Bimbo would have breakfast.

Bimbo would also leave Tito at lunchtime. He always came back with a scrap of bread, meat, or fruit. Sometimes he'd bring a raisin-and-sugar cake that Tito especially loved. At suppertime, Bimbo brought the smallest meal. Food was
20 harder to get when many people were around.

Tito didn't feel sorry for himself. He couldn't see Pompeii, but his ears and nose told him what was happening.

The forum in the center of town was the best place to find news. Many kinds of shops, the biggest temples, and
25 the town hall were there. All of these public buildings were new. They had replaced buildings that an earthquake had brought down.

---

1. **chariots** (CHAR ee uhts): two-wheeled carts pulled by horses. Chariots were used a long time ago for war, races, and parades.
2. **emperor** (EM puhr uhr): the highest ruler of a government.
3. **wonders:** things that cause surprise and admiration.

"The Dog of Pompeii" adapted from *The Donkey of God* by Louis Untermeyer. Copyright 1932 by Harcourt Brace & Company. Retold by Holt, Rinehart and Winston. Reproduced by permission of **Laurence S. Untermeyer on behalf of the Estate of Louis Untermeyer, Norma Anchin Untermeyer, c/o Professional Publishing Services Company.**

Tito did not remember the earthquake because it had happened years ago when he was a baby. That earthquake had been a light one. Weak buildings had fallen down, but a more beautiful Pompeii had replaced the old one.

People wondered what caused earthquakes. Some said they happened to teach people a lesson. Others said that the earth shook when the gods showed their anger. Everyone had a different explanation.

This afternoon, people in the forum were talking again about the earthquake. Tito's ears led him to where the talk was loudest.

"I'll tell you, there won't be another earthquake in my lifetime. Earthquakes are like lightning. They never strike twice in the same place," one voice said.

A stranger's voice answered, "Do they not? Remember those two towns that were ruined three times? And were the people not warned? Does that column of smoke above Vesuvius mean nothing?"

"That?" said another voice. "That smoke is always there."

"Yes, yes," cut in the stranger's voice. "But the column of smoke seems higher than usual. It's thick, and it spreads like a tree. We have a saying where I come from. It's this: *Those who will not listen to men must be taught by the gods.* I say no more. But I leave a last warning. Notice when the smoke tree above Vesuvius grows to the shape of a pine. Then, watch out for your lives."

Tito heard the stranger walk quickly away. He wondered what the stranger meant. Bimbo tilted his head as if he were also thinking about it. But by nightfall the argument had been forgotten. The town was celebrating Caesar's birthday. Everyone was in a holiday mood. Tito and Bimbo went to the theater. Tito listened to the play. Then they went to the city

Your TURN

CREDIBLE CHARACTERS

In ancient Roman times, the forum (line 36) was the most important public place. Which places in modern towns are similar to the forum? What kinds of things do people talk about there?

_____

_____

_____

Here's HOW

MAKING INFERENCES

In lines 36-53, I wonder why most of the people are talking about earthquakes and not volcanoes. Aren't volcanoes dangerous, too? But maybe the people think earthquakes are worse because they shake the earth. That would cause buildings to fall. It would also be hard to run away if the earth were shaking.

Here's HOW

VOCABULARY

My teacher explained that *Vesuvius* in line 45 is the name of a volcano near Pompeii. It is pronounced "vuh SOO vee uhs."

THE DOG OF POMPEII 137

Your TURN

MAKING INFERENCES

In lines 65–67, where do you think this "thick fog" came from, and why?

_____
_____
_____
_____
_____

Here's HOW

CREDIBLE CHARACTERS

True-to-life characters are not perfect. Like real people, they sometimes show poor judgment. For example, Tito makes a mistake when he doesn't pay attention to Bimbo's strange behavior. I would probably have made the same mistake. It's impossible to know exactly what will happen before it happens!

---

60 wall where people watched a pretend sea battle with ships on fire. The cheers and shouts excited both Tito and Bimbo.

The next morning, Bimbo brought Tito two raisin-and-sugar cakes for breakfast. Bimbo's thumping tail seemed to be trying to tell Tito something. But Tito did not know what 65 it was. He felt sleepy. A thick fog stuck in his throat and made him cough. He walked all the way to the sea gate[4] to breathe in the sea air. But even the salty air seemed smoky.

That night, Tito did not sleep well. He dreamed of ships in the forum and of being lost, with people marching over him. 70 Finally, he was being pulled over rough pavement. He woke to find that Bimbo was pulling him. The dog had dragged Tito to his feet and was pushing the boy along. Where, Tito did not know. He was still half asleep. The hot, heavy air was hard to breathe. Powder stung his nose and burned his eyes.

75 Then Tito began to hear sounds. Hisses, groans, and cries came from under the earth. They sounded like a dying animal. Now he could feel the earth jerk. Tito fell against a fountain.

Hot water from the fountain splashed in Tito's face. He 80 was more awake now. Helped up by Bimbo, Tito hurried on. Now they heard louder, human sounds. A few people, then many, rushed by. Then Tito could hear a roar like the fall of a forest of trees. He could hear the crash of thunder and houses falling around them. By a miracle, Tito and Bimbo escaped to 85 the forum. It was safer here, and they rested awhile.

Tito had no idea of the time of day. His empty stomach told him it was past noon, but hunger didn't matter. Nothing seemed to matter. Tito was too tired to walk, but Bimbo pulled him on. And it was just in time. The ground of the 90 forum had begun to split. The columns of the temple to

---

4. sea gate: gate in a city wall leading to the sea.

Jupiter[5] came down. The world seemed to be ending. Walking was not fast enough. They must run. But Tito was lost and didn't know where to go. Bimbo pulled him so hard his clothes nearly came off. Had Bimbo gone mad? What did he want?

Then suddenly Tito understood. Bimbo was telling him the way out. They had to get to the sea gate. That was the only place away from the falling buildings and shaking ground. Bimbo guided Tito through the streets. They ran through the screaming crowds toward the sea gate.

But everyone was headed that way. And it was getting harder to breathe. The air was all dust. Pebbles the size of beans fell on Tito's head. The mountain of Vesuvius had been turned inside out. Tito remembered what the stranger had said: "Those who will not listen to men must be taught by the gods." The people of Pompeii had not listened. Now they were being taught—if it was not too late.

Suddenly it seemed too late for Tito. He fell at the side of the road. Bimbo licked Tito's face and hands, but Tito did not move. Then Bimbo did the last thing he could—the last thing he wanted to do. He bit Tito deep in the arm. Tito cried in pain and jumped up. Then he pounded on with Bimbo barking at his heels. At last Tito reached the sea gate and felt the sand under him. Then he fainted.

He awoke to feel someone carrying him. "Bimbo!" he called. "Bimbo!" But Bimbo was gone.

Tito heard voices saying, "The poor boy must be crazy."

They put Tito into a boat. He could hear oars splash as the boat rode over the waves. Tito was safe, but he kept calling, "Bimbo!" He cried and cried, but no one could comfort him.

---

5. **Jupiter** (JOO piht uhr): the highest god in the religion of the Romans.

Your TURN

MAKING INFERENCES

In lines 97–100, Tito and Bimbo are rushing toward the sea gate. One reason is to avoid falling buildings. What is another good reason to escape to the sea?

_____
_____
_____
_____
_____

Here's HOW

CREDIBLE CHARACTERS

Bimbo is gone! Where did he go? Bimbo cared so much for Tito. He took care of him. Tito and Bimbo loved each other deeply. This is too sad. I can't stand it! I don't understand why Bimbo left.

THE DOG OF POMPEII 139

Your Turn

MAKING INFERENCES

Re-read lines 130–137. Why do you think Bimbo left Tito after taking him to safety? What did Bimbo go to do?

_____
_____
_____
_____
_____
_____
_____

Your Turn

CREDIBLE CHARACTERS

Do you find what Bimbo did believable? Why or why not?

_____
_____
_____
_____
_____
_____
_____

Eighteen hundred years passed. Scientists were digging up the ancient city of Pompeii. The eruption had killed over two thousand people, but many things had been saved in the ashes.

"Look here," one scientist called to his assistant. "I think we've found what is left of a building that looks like a bakery. And what do you think I found under this heap of ashes? It's the bones of a dog!"

"Amazing," said his assistant. "You'd think a dog would have known enough to run away. Is that a stone between his teeth?

"No," the scientist answered. "It must have come from this bakery. It looks to me like a cake. And those things that look like pebbles are raisins. It's a raisin cake over two thousand years old! I wonder what made the dog want it at such a moment."

"I wonder," murmured[6] the assistant.

---

6. **murmured** (MUHR muhrd): said in a voice so quiet it could barely be heard.

Making Inferences

As you read "The Dog of Pompeii," you made **many inferences,** or educated guesses. Now, complete the chart below. Read each question. Then, write down what you already know to help you answer the question. Next, find details in the story that help you answer the question. Finally, write your answer to the question—your **inference**—in the last column. Number 2 has been completed for you.

Question	What I Know	Story Details	My Inference
1. Why are Tito and Bimbo so close to one another? (lines 6–15)			
2. Why is Bimbo acting so strangely? (lines 62–95)	Some dogs can sense natural disasters before they happen.	The man warns about the column of smoke above the volcano.	Maybe Bimbo is sensing that the volcano is about to erupt.
3. Where does the thick fog come from? Why? (lines 65–67)			
4. Why do Tito and Bimbo rush toward the sea? (lines 97–100)			
5. Why did Bimbo leave Tito after taking him to safety? (lines 115–137)			

Pet Adoption Application

Reading Skill: Understanding Applications

What is an **application**? An application is a form. The form has lines and boxes to record important information. When might you need to fill out an application?

- when you start classes at a new school
- when you join a club or a team
- when you go to summer camp
- when you apply for a job
- when you are ready for a driver's license

An application must be complete and correct. If it isn't, important information gets lost. Here are some tips to help you fill out applications.

Application Tips

- Read all the instructions before you begin to write.
- Take your time, and write neatly.
- Follow directions about which lines and boxes to fill in.
- Check to see if you need to sign the application.

Into the Application

Taking care of a pet is a big responsibility. That's why animal shelters allow only adults to adopt pets. Now you will read a Pet Adoption Application. It asks many questions. The shelter must be sure that each pet gets a safe home. What information does the shelter need to know?

PET ADOPTION
Application

Here's HOW

UNDERSTANDING APPLICATIONS

This form has so many boxes! I should start at the top. It says, "Instructions." Oh, look—I only have to fill in the white boxes.

Your TURN

UNDERSTANDING APPLICATIONS

The application asks if the adopter has a fenced yard. Find this question, and circle it. Why is this information important?

_____

_____

Your TURN

UNDERSTANDING APPLICATIONS

The application asks for references. A reference is a person who can answer questions like, "Is the adopter a responsible person?" or "Can she take care of a pet?" Why might the shelter ask these questions?

_____

_____

INSTRUCTIONS: Adopter, print carefully in **WHITE AREAS ONLY**—do not write in shaded areas.

Pet Adoption Application

❏ Puppy ❏ Kitten ❏ Dog ❏ Cat

Date / /	Single Adoption	Double Adoption	Age	Program	H D	T O	Adoption Number
Day	Time ❏ AM ❏ PM	Breed	Color	MTA MTD	L G	R circle one	

Sex — ❏ Mr. ❏ Mrs. ❏ Ms. ❏ Miss ❏ Mr. & Mrs.

Voluntary Contribution — Size: S___ M___ L___ — Spay/Neuter

Adopter's Last Name   First Name

Cash	$	❏ Pure	❏ Mix	Vaccine Type	Street Address Apt. #
Check	$		Pet's Name	Vaccine Date	
D V M A circle one	$			Rabies Tag	City State/Zip Code
Credit A/R	($)	ASC Int.	No.	Rabies Date	

Total Voluntary Contribution $ _____
X _____

Wormed / Med. Given / NMR / Tech. App.

Home Phone   Business Phone
(   )   -   (   )   -

Name of Reference	Address	City	State	Telephone	ID Source
				( ) -	❏ Yes ❏ No
				( ) -	D V ❏ Yes / M A ❏ No

1. WHOM IS THE PET FOR? Self____ Gift____ For whom?_____ Adopter's age:____

2. IF YOU'RE SINGLE: Do you live alone? Yes____ No____ Do you live with family? Yes____ No____
   Do you work? Yes____ No____ What are your hours?_____

   IF YOU'RE MARRIED: Do you both work? Yes____ No____ Husband's hours:_____
   Wife's hours:_____ How many children at home?_____ Ages:_____, _____, _____
   Who will be responsible for the pet? Husband____ Wife____ Children____ Other_____

3. DO YOU: OWN ❏ RENT ❏ HOUSE ❏ APT. ❏ Floor #____ Elevator in the building? Yes____ No____
   (CHECK ONE)   (CHECK ONE)
   If renting, does your lease allow pets? Yes___ No___ Are you moving? Yes___ No___ When?_____
   Do you have use of a private yard? Yes___ No___ Is it fenced? Yes___ No___ Fence height:_____
   Where will your pet be kept?_____ / _____ Any allergy to pets? Yes___ No___
                                DAYTIME   NIGHTTIME

4. DO YOU HAVE OTHER PETS NOW? Yes____ No____ Breed:_____
   Where did you get the pet?_____ How long have you had it?_____

   HAVE YOU EVER HAD A PET BEFORE? Yes____ No____ Breed:_____
   How long did you have the pet?_____ What happened to the pet?_____
   Have you ever adopted from this shelter? Yes___ No___ Where is the pet now?_____

5. YOUR OCCUPATION:_____ Business Phone: (   )_____
   Company:_____ Supervisor's Name:_____

VET'S NAME	CITY, STATE	ZIP CODE

Adopter's Signature:

North Shore Animal League Pet Adoption Application. Copyright © 2000 by North Shore Animal League. Reproduced by permission of **North Shore Animal League, Port Washington, New York.**

Veterinarian Registration Form

A **registration form** is a kind of application. It collects important information about you and your family. Here is a registration form for a pet. Pets need care from pet doctors called veterinarians. Dogs and cats need shots and yearly check-ups.

Fill out the registration form below. Remember the tips you learned! If you don't have a pet, that's okay. You can pretend.

Hall Street Veterinary Office

Help us help your pet. Fill out every line clearly. Sign the form at the bottom.

About You

Your Name: _____ Today's Date: _____

Your Address (Street, City, and Zip Code): _____

_____

Your Phone Number: _____

About Your Pet

Your Pet's Name: _____

Check one: Dog _____ Cat _____ Bird _____ Your Pet's Age: _____

Has your pet been sick or hurt? Check one: Yes _____ No _____

If you checked Yes, tell us how your pet was sick or hurt.

_____

What kind of food does your pet eat?

_____

If this information is correct, please sign the form on the line below. Thank you!

_____
(signature)

PHOTO CREDITS

Abbreviations used: (l) left, (r) right, (t) top, (c) center, (b) bottom, (tl) top left, (tr) top right, (cl) center left, (cr) center right, (bc) bottom center, (bl) bottom left, (br) bottom right, (bkgd) background.

Page xii (border), 1–6, Getty Images/Stone; 17–27, © Anatoly Sapronenkov/SuperStock; 30 (border), Digital Image copyright © 2005 PhotoDisc; 30 (border), Courtesy of The San Diego Museum of Man, San Diego, California; 31 (bkgd), Digital Image copyright © 2005 PhotoDisc; 31 (b), 32–35, Courtesy of The San Diego Museum of Man, San Diego, California; 39–40 Kansas State Historical Society, Topeka; 50–52, Library of Congress; 54–55 (bkgd), Digital Image copyright © 2005 PhotoDisc; 55 (c), 56, Michael Newman/PhotoEdit; 64–65 (bkgd), Digital Image copyright © 2005 PhotoDisc; 65 (l), Mary Kate Denny/PhotoEdit; 65 (r), Robin L. Sachs/PhotoEdit; 66 (l), Mary Kate Denny/PhotoEdit; 66 (r), Robin L. Sachs/PhotoEdit; 66 (bkgd), 74–75 (bkgd), Digital Image copyright © 2005 PhotoDisc; 75 (tl, tr, & bc), 76, Courtesy of Free The Children; 79 (t), Library of Congress; 79 (b), Courtesy of the National Afro-American Museum and Cultural Center, Wilberforce, Ohio; 80 (t), Library of Congress; 89–92, Museo Archeologico, Syracuse, Sicily, Italy. Scala/Art Resource, NY; 94–95 (bkgd), Digital Image copyright © 2005 PhotoDisc; 95 (c), 96, RobertStock.com; 97 (c), Ralph A. Reinhold/Index Stock Imagery, Inc.; 97 (bkgd), Digital Image copyright © 2005 PhotoDisc; 98, Ralph A. Reinhold/Index Stock Imagery, Inc.; 100–101, Digital Image copyright © 2005 PhotoDisc; 101, Boy by the Sea (1995) by Jonathan Green, Naples, Florida. Oil on canvas (18" X 17"). Photograph by Tim Stamm; 102–103, Digital Image copyright © 2005 PhotoDisc; 106 (border), Tony Freeman/PhotoEdit; 107 (c), The Granger Collection, New York; 107 (bkgd), Tony Freeman/PhotoEdit; 108–110, The Granger Collection, New York; 113 (tr), National Archives (NARA) Photo No. 111-B-6135; 113 (c), The Granger Collection, New York; 114–116, National Archives (NARA) Photo No. 111-B-6135; 118–119 (bkgd), Digital Image copyright © 2005 PhotoDisc; 119 (cl & cr), 120–121, The Granger Collection, New York; 124–125 (bkgd), Digital Image copyright © 2005 PhotoDisc; 125 (cr), © Michael Neuman/PictureQuest; 125 (cl), Digital Image copyright © 2005 PhotoDisc; 126, © Michael Neuman/PictureQuest; 128 (border), 129–132, Lester Lefkowitz/Getty Images/FPG International; 142–144, Digital Image copyright © 2005 PhotoDisc.

AUTHOR AND TITLE INDEX

A
Alexander, Lloyd 9
All Aboard with Thomas Garrett 106
Andersen, Hans Christian 59
Angelou, Maya 100

B
Bamba, La 82
Baucis and Philemon 68
Bracelet, The 42
Bridegroom, The 16
Bringing Tang Home 95
Brother 100

C
Coolidge, Olivia 69, 88

D
Day, Nancy 51
De Lange, Flo Ota 39
Dog of Pompeii, The 134
Dygard, Thomas J. 1

E
Emperor's New Clothes, The 58
Everybody Is Different, but the Same Too 54

F
Freedman, Russell 112

G
Getting Leftovers Back on the Table 124

H
Henderson, Sheri 97

J
John Henry 128
Just Once 1

K
Koenig, Louis W. 118

L
Lincoln's Humor 118

M
Medusa's Head 88
Miller, Alice P. 106
Mysterious Mr. Lincoln, The 112

N
Nilou 55

O
One Child's Labor of Love 74

P
Pet Adoption Application 142
Pushkin, Alexander 17

R
Rockliff, Mara 65, 79, 124

S
Separate but Never Equal 78
60 Minutes, from 75
Soto, Gary 82
Spadafori, Gina 95
Stone, The 8

AUTHOR AND TITLE INDEX

T
Ta-Na-E-Ka 30

U
Uchida, Yoshiko 43
Uniform Style 64
Untermeyer, Louis 134

W
Wartime Mistakes, Peacetime Apologies 50
Where the Heart Is 97
Whitebird, Mary 31
Wind People, The 38